ITALY

PHOTOGRAPHS BY ELIZABETH KRAMER

THIS IS PART OF THE VISITING SERIES.

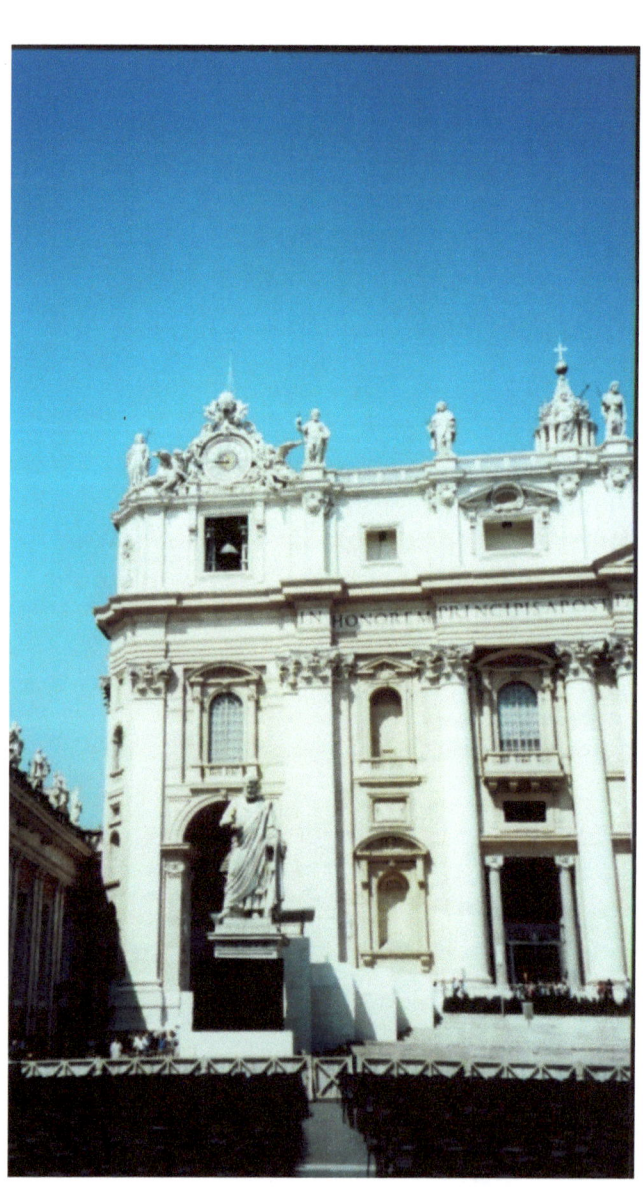

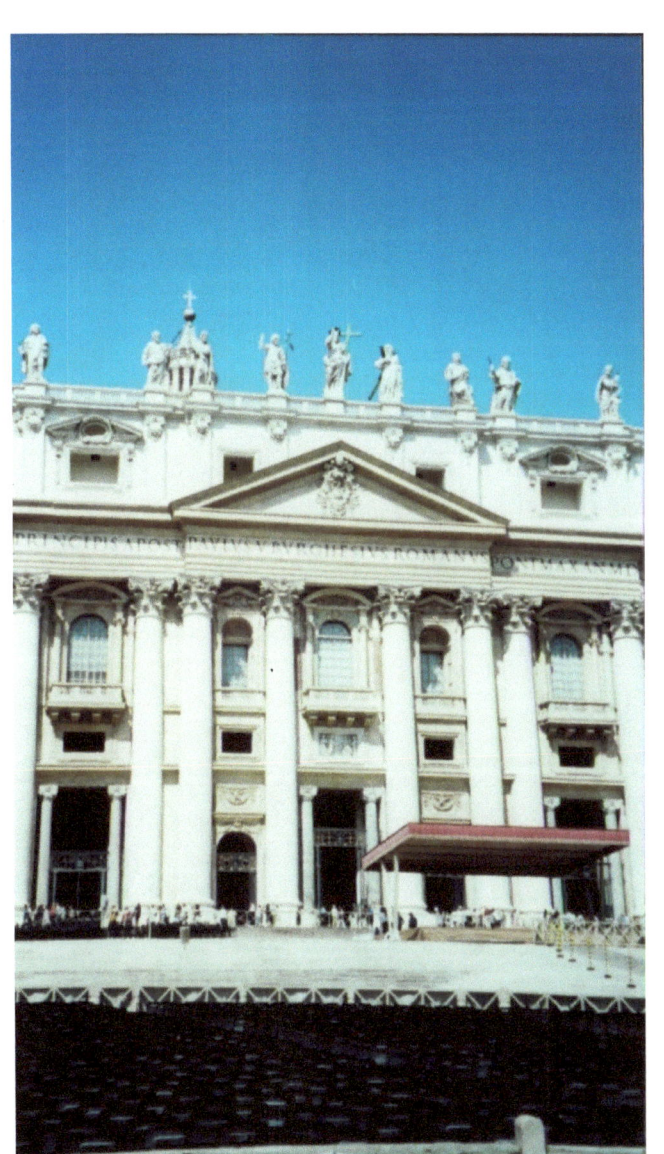

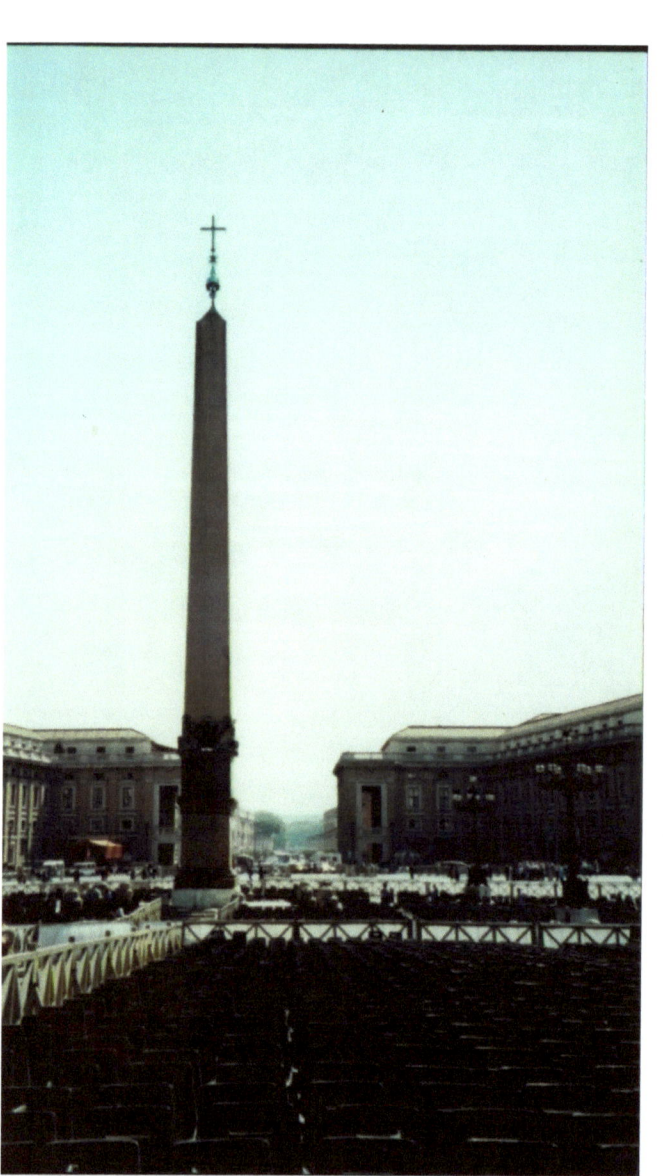

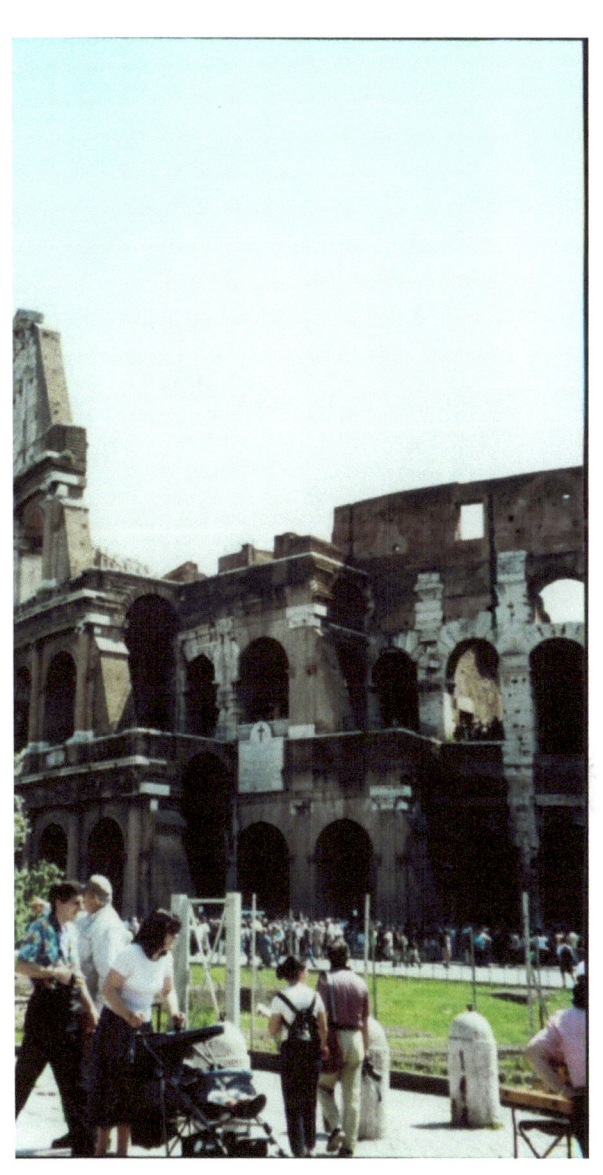

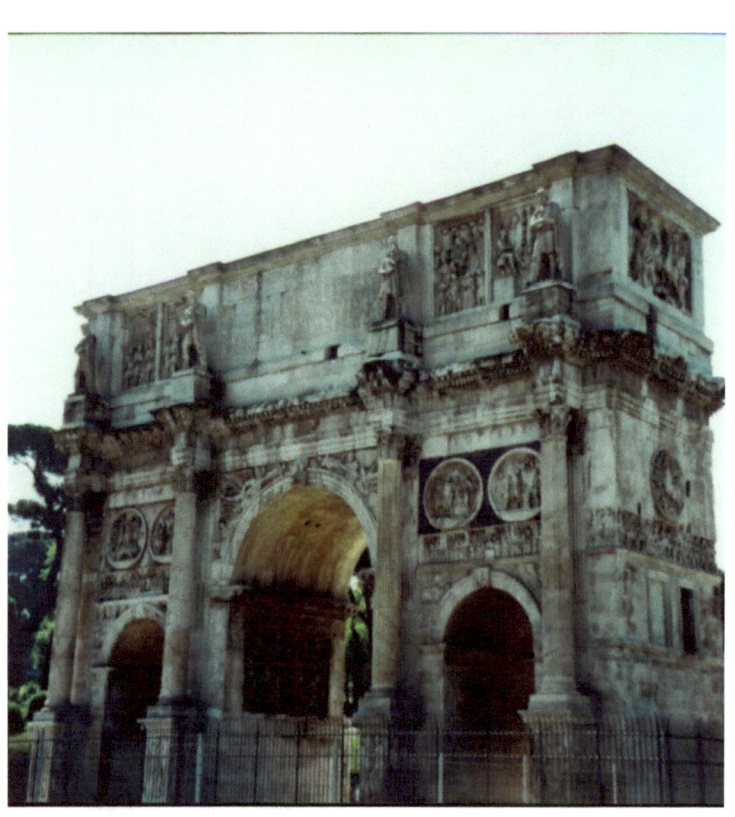

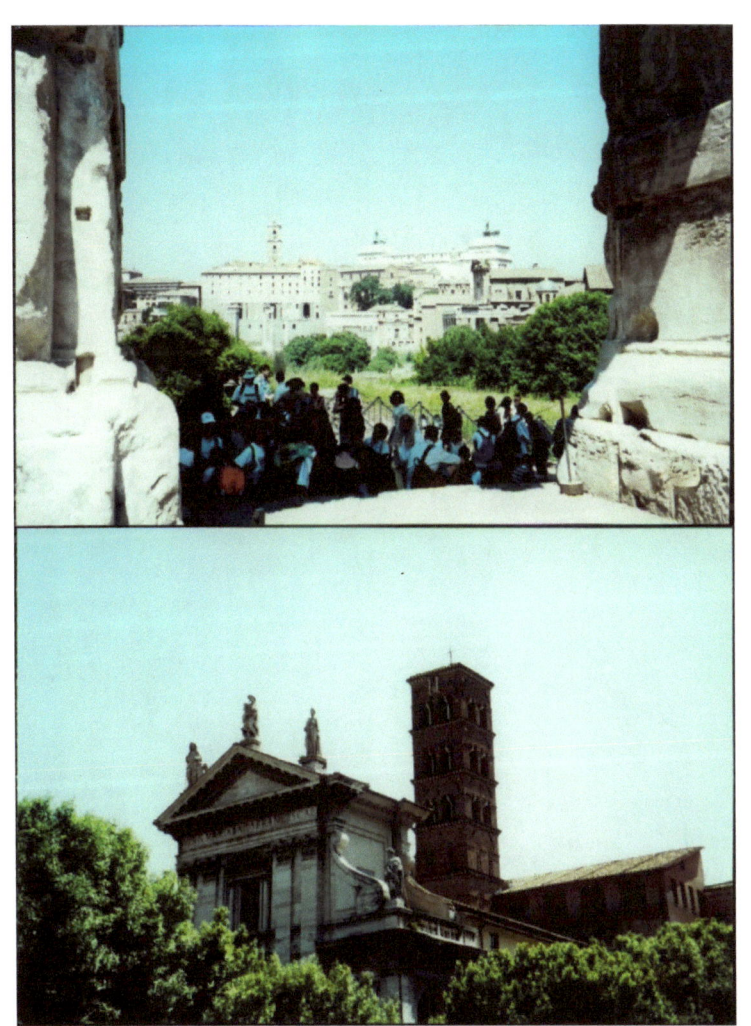

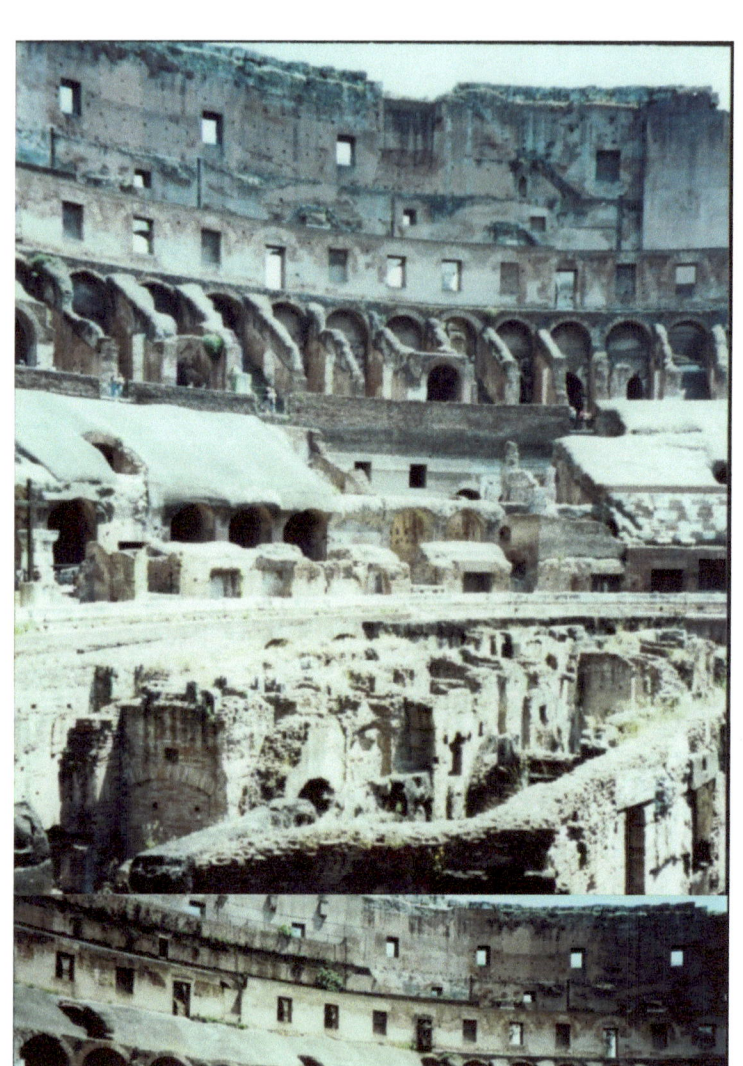

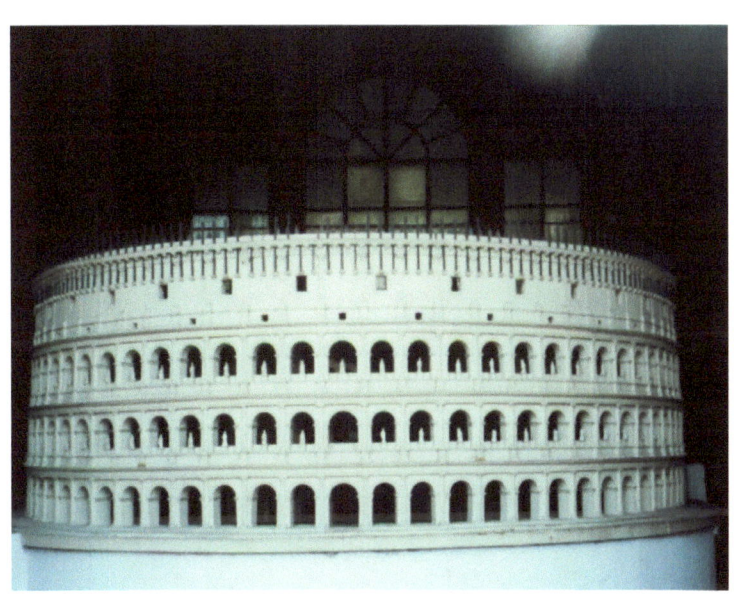

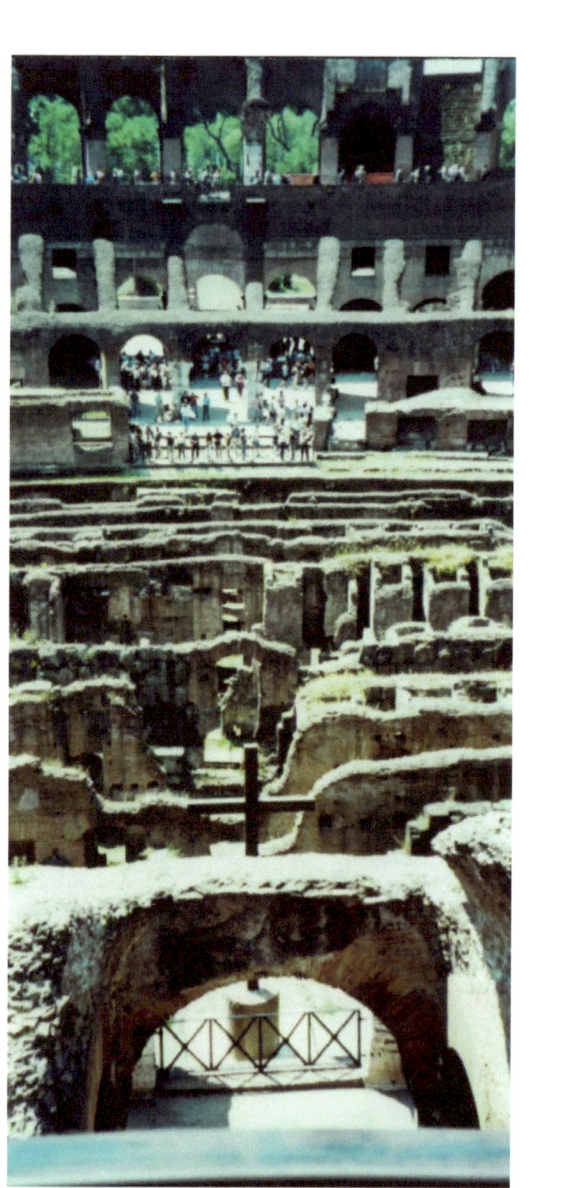

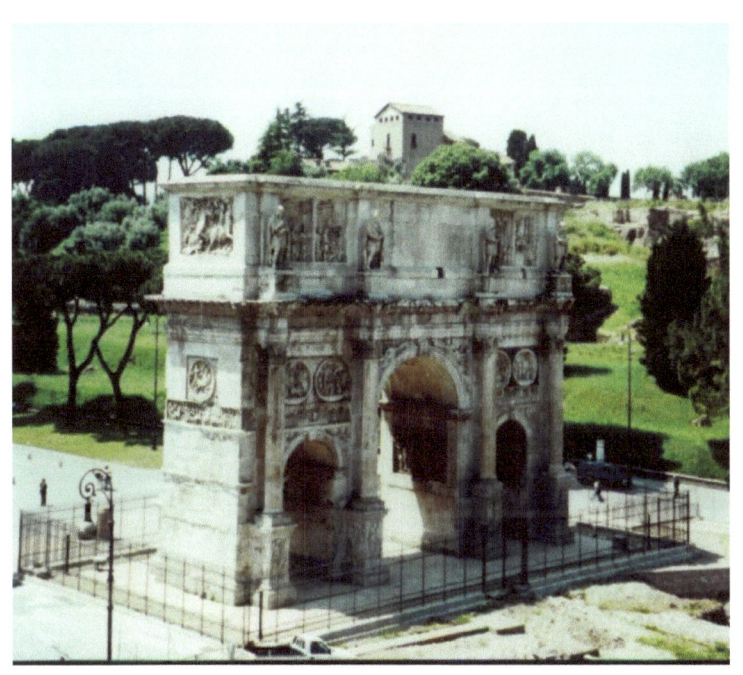

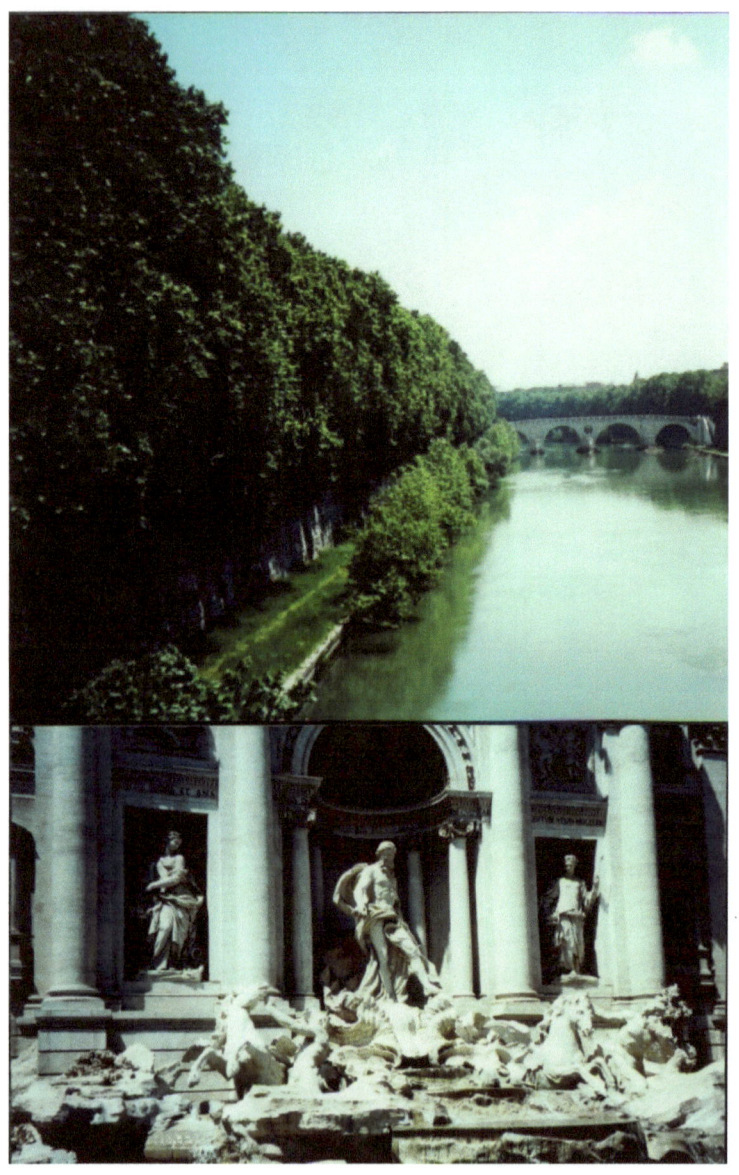

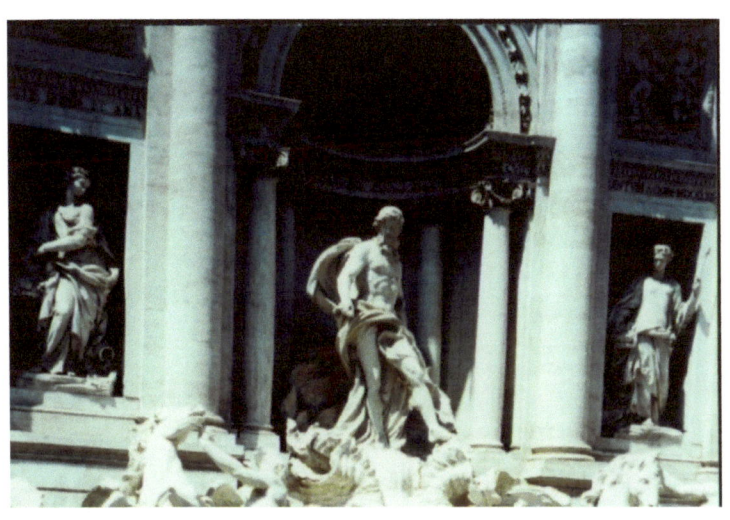

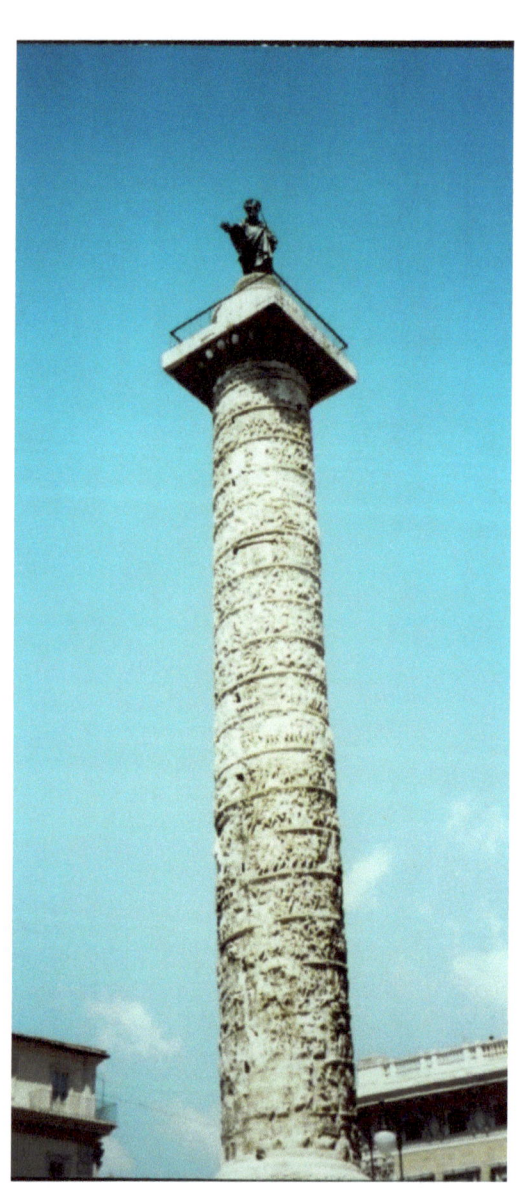

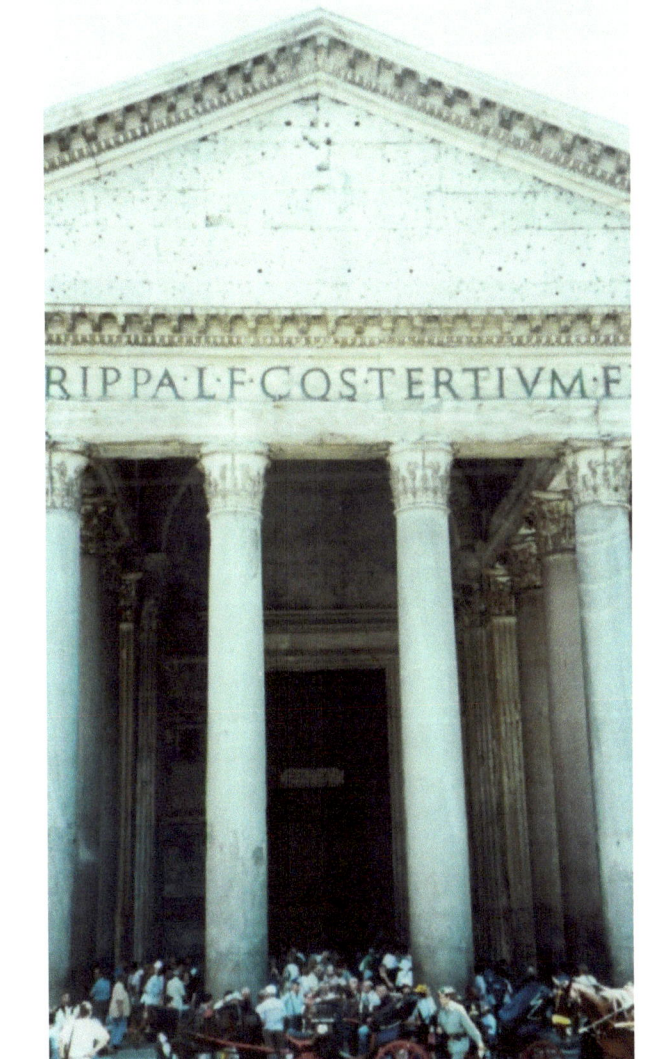

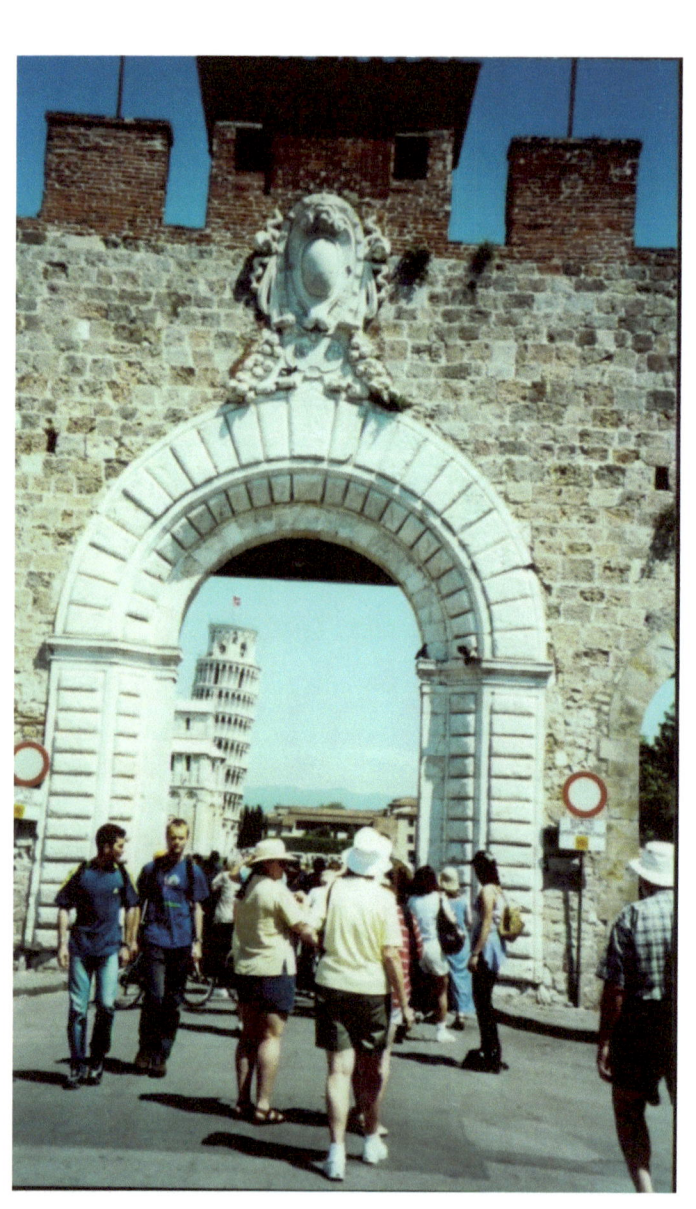

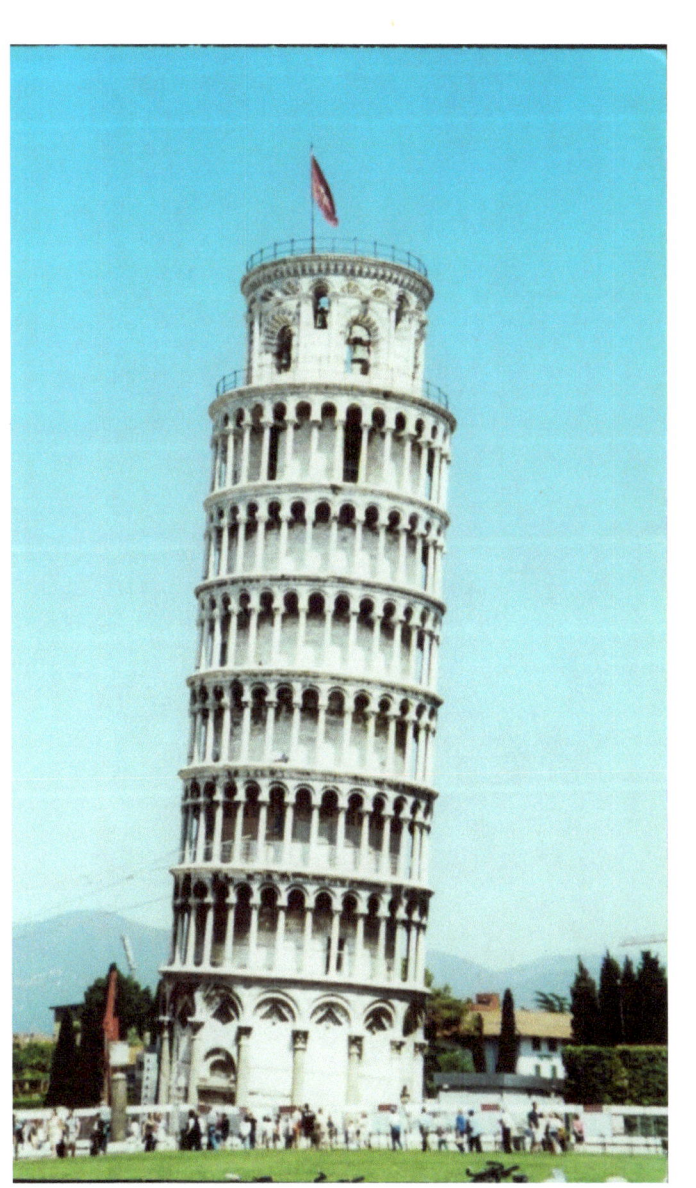

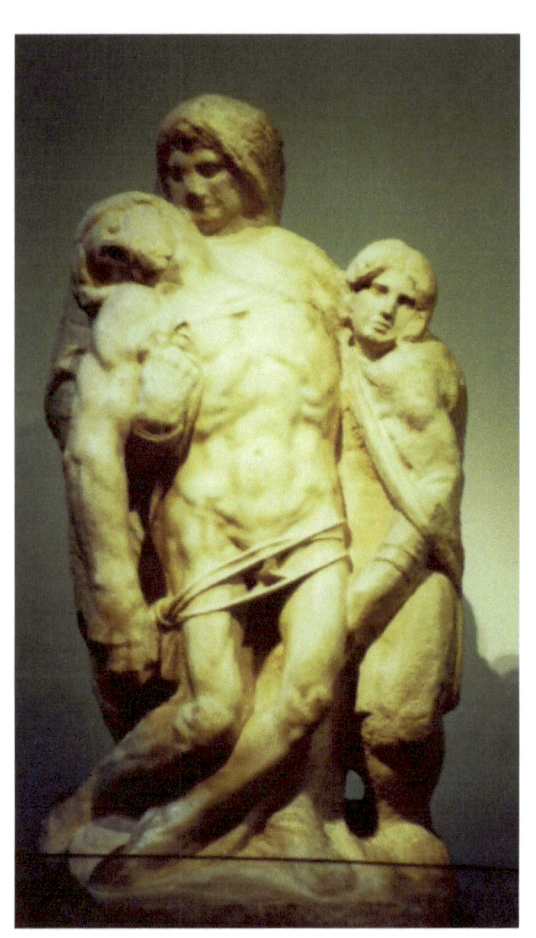

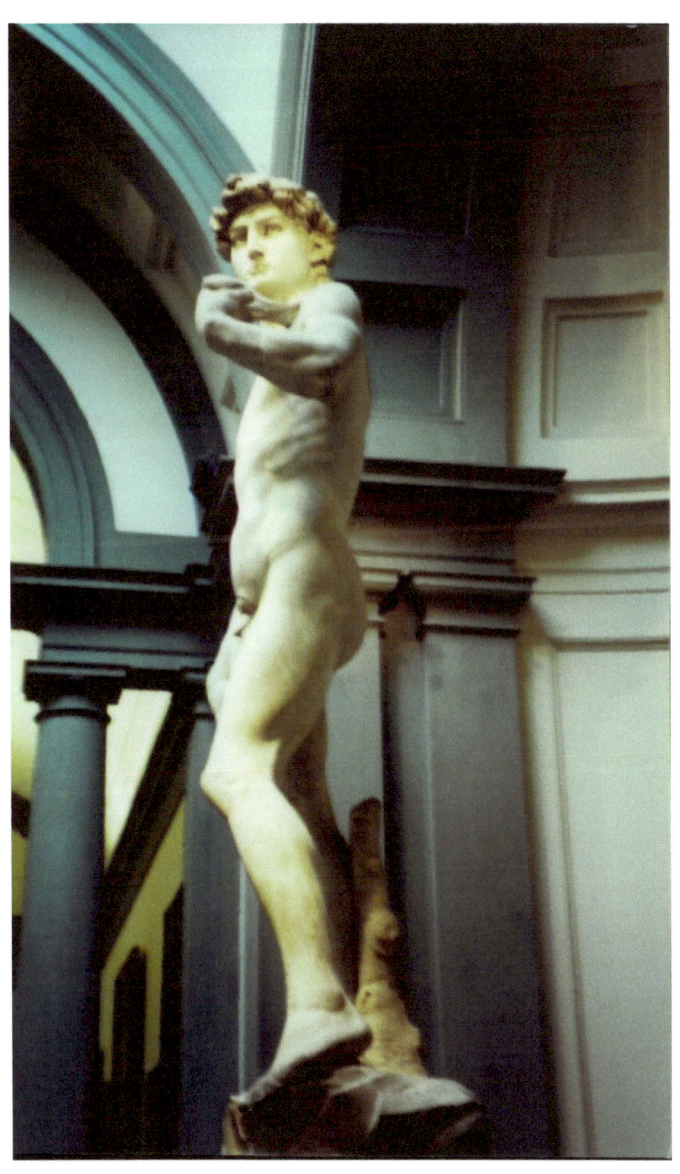

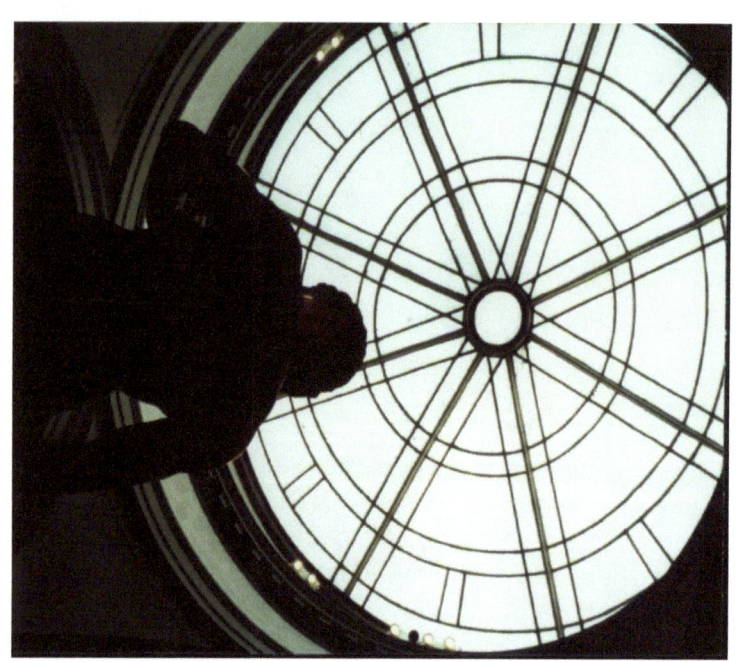

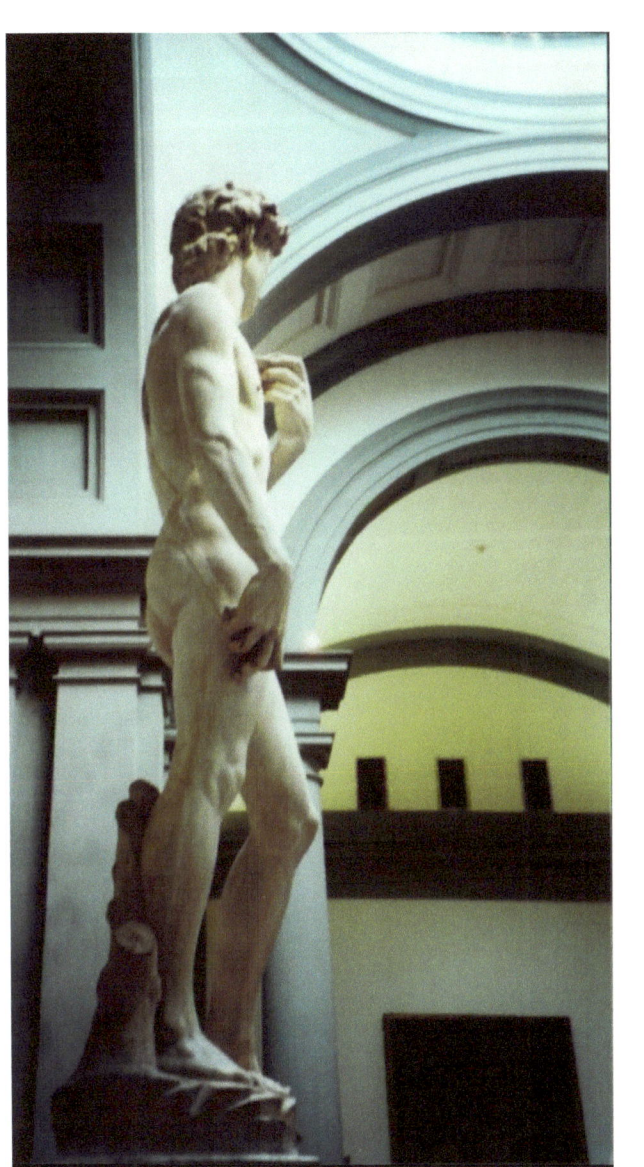

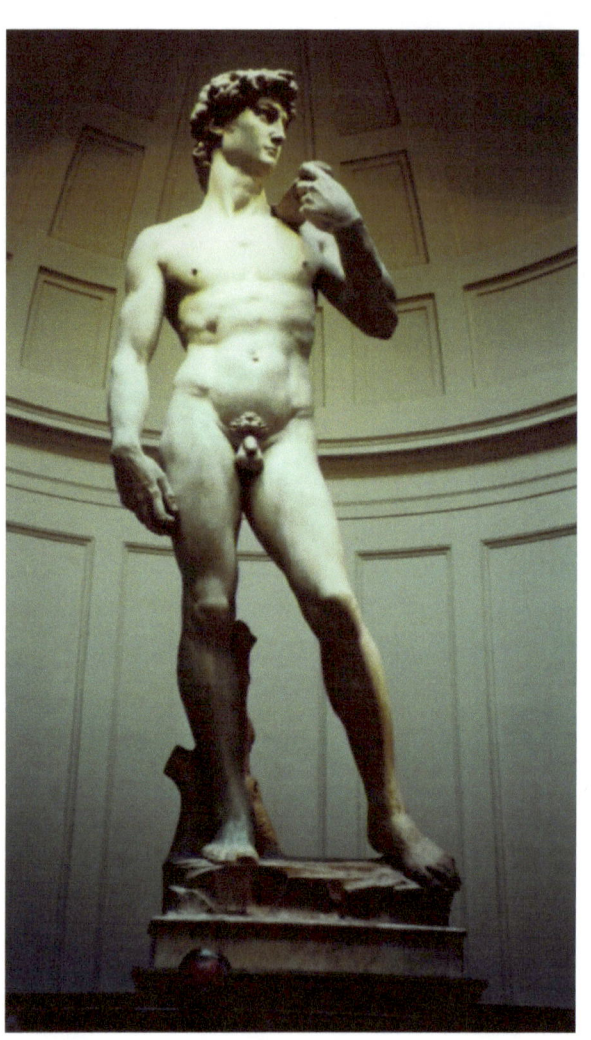

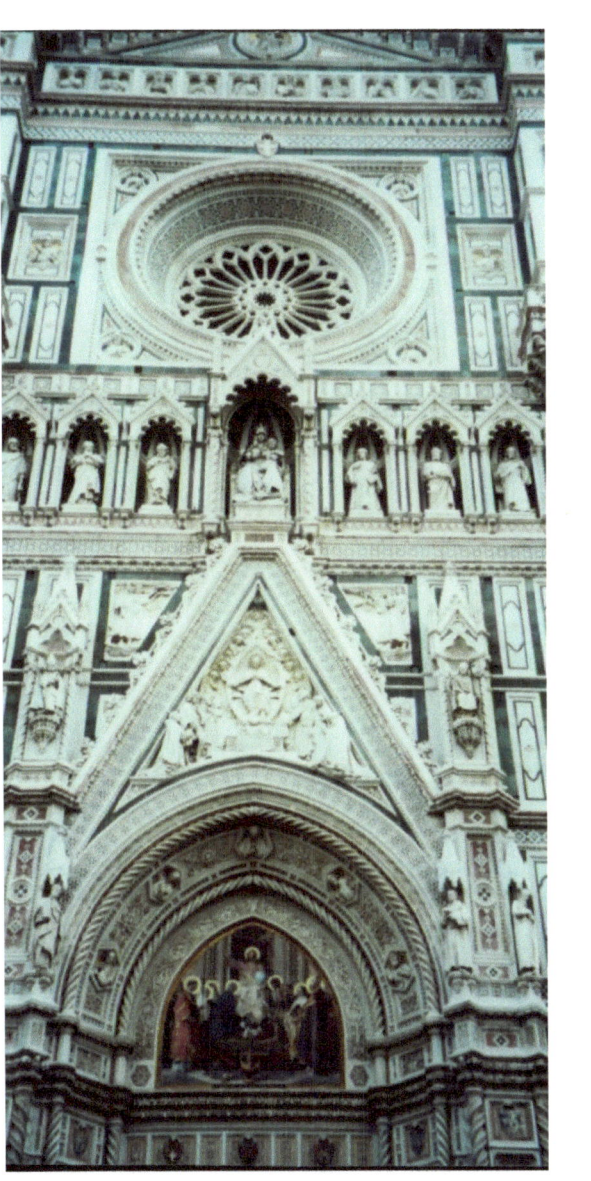

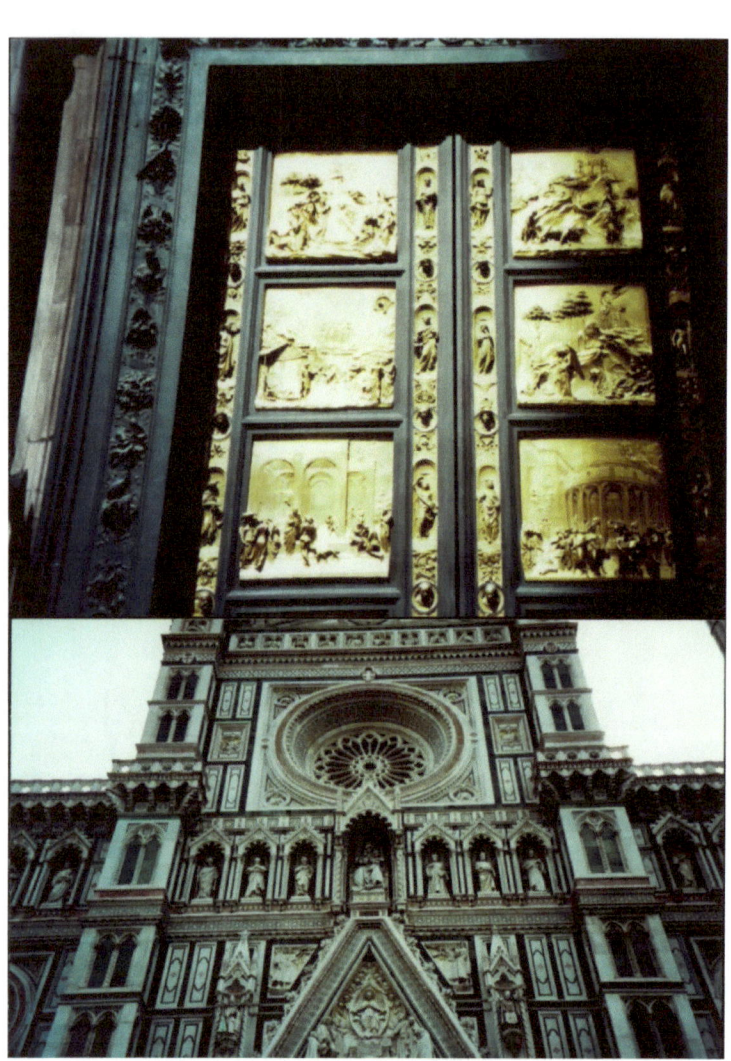

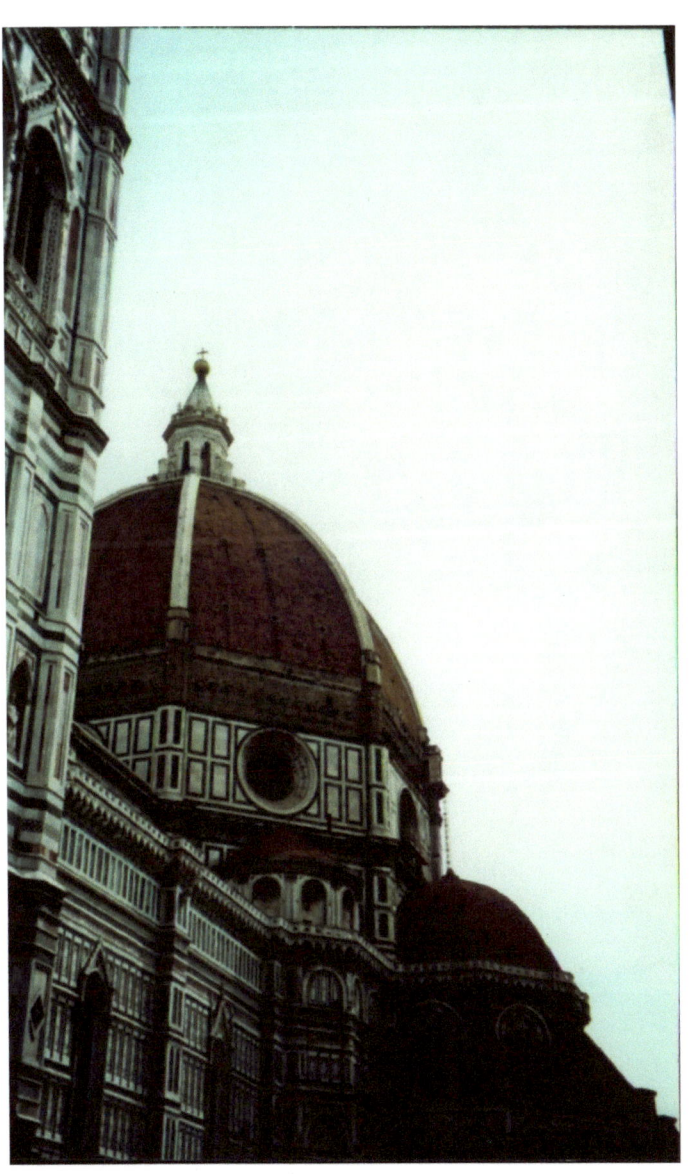

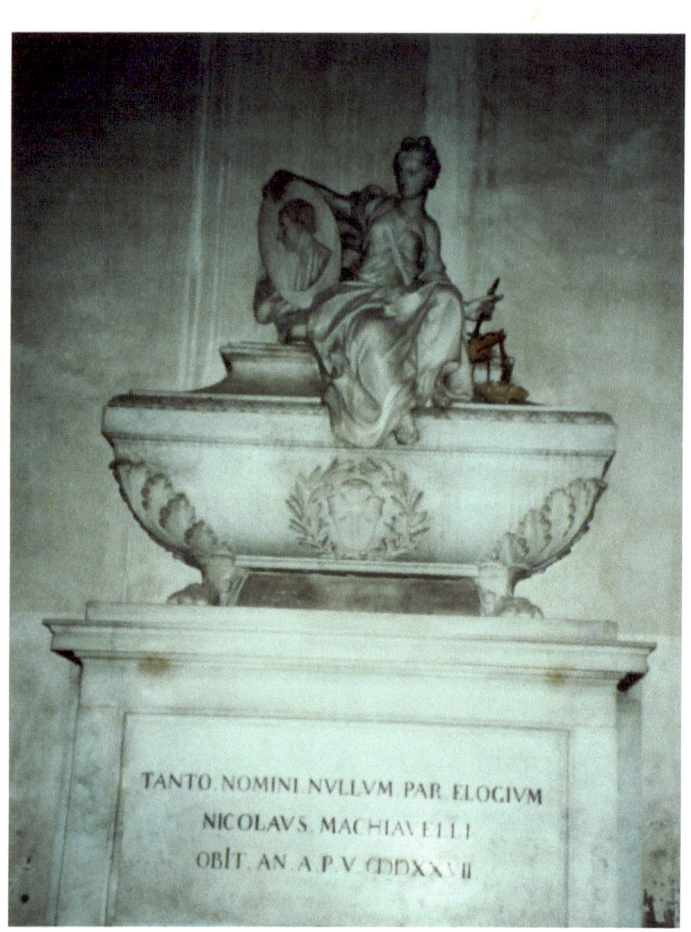

TANTO. NOMINI. NVLLVM. PAR. ELOGIVM
NICOLAVS. MACHIAVELLI
OBIT. AN. A. P. V. CIƆIƆXXVII

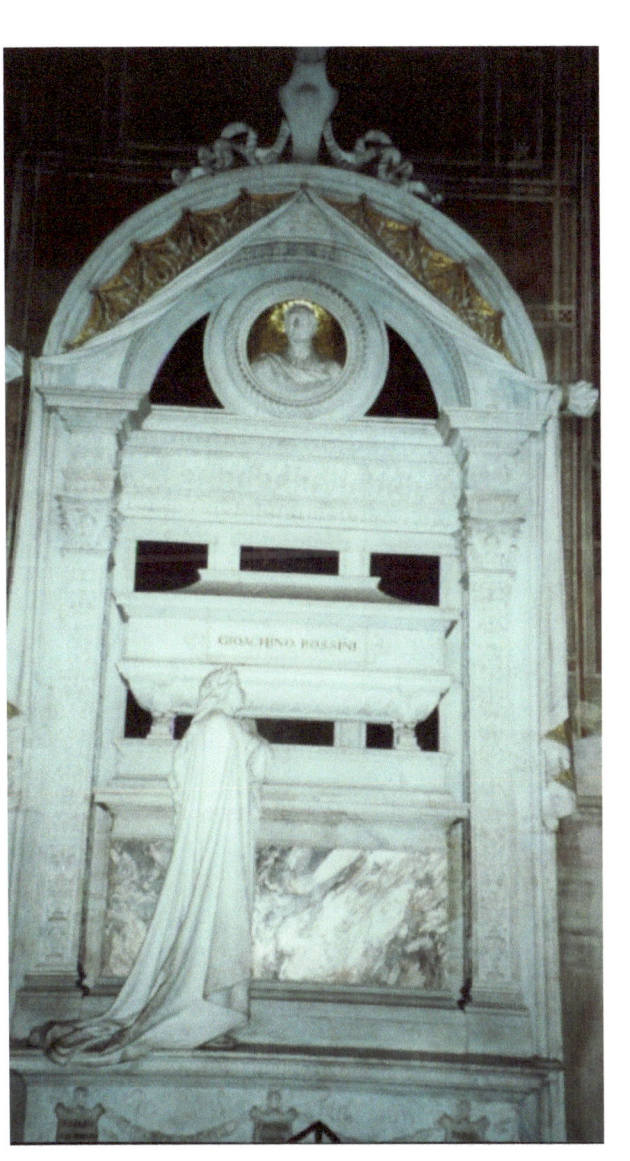

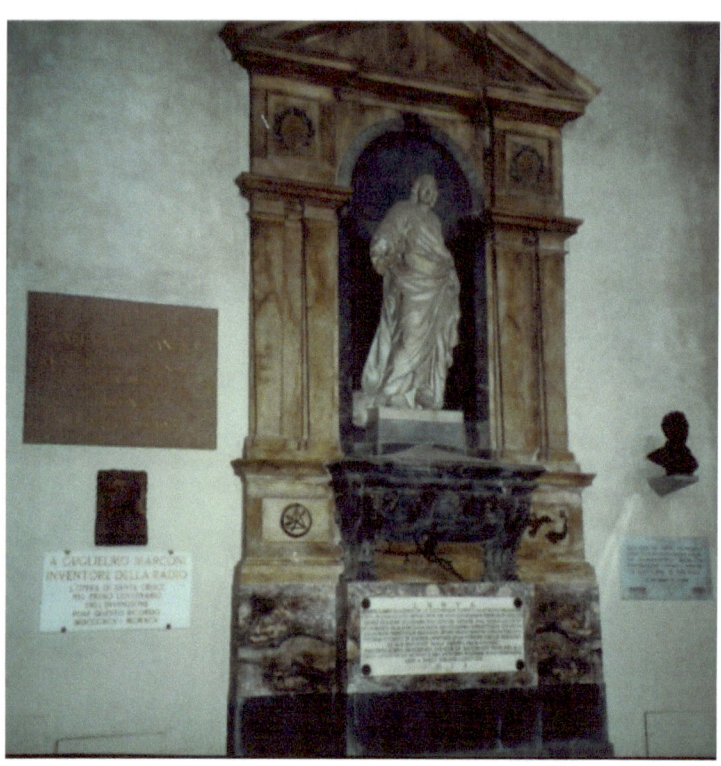

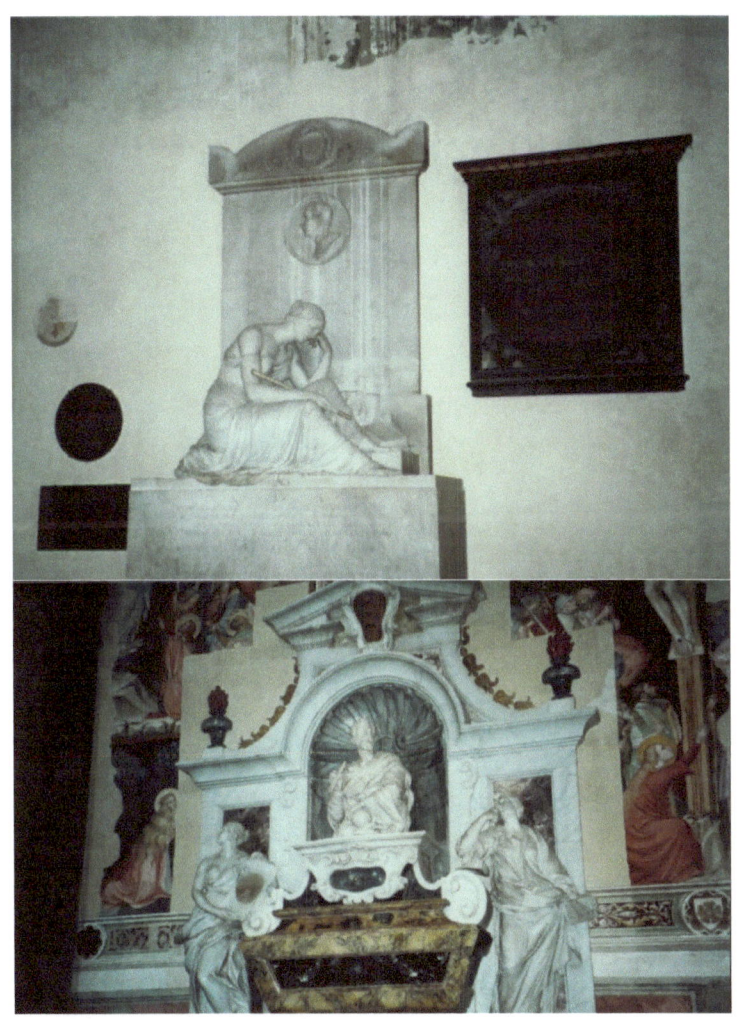

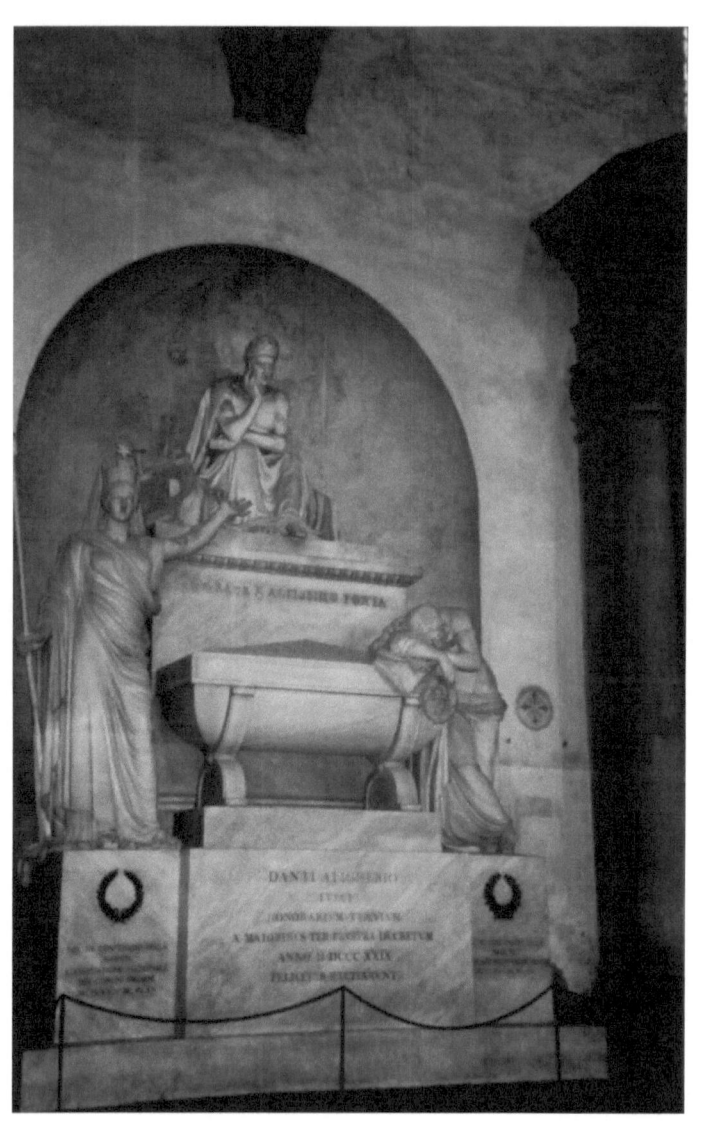

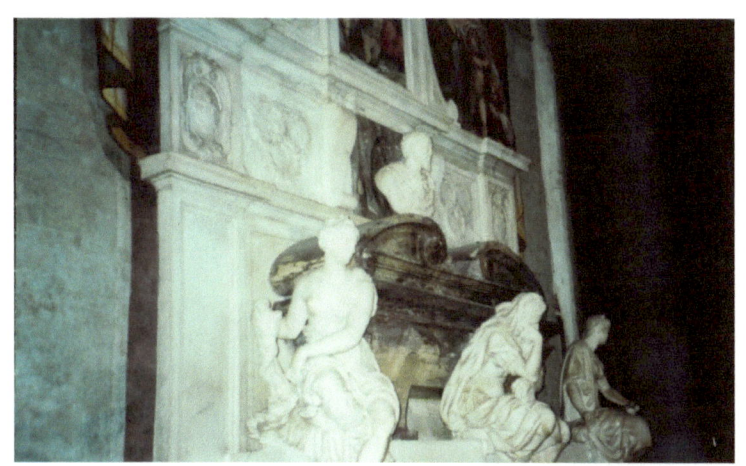

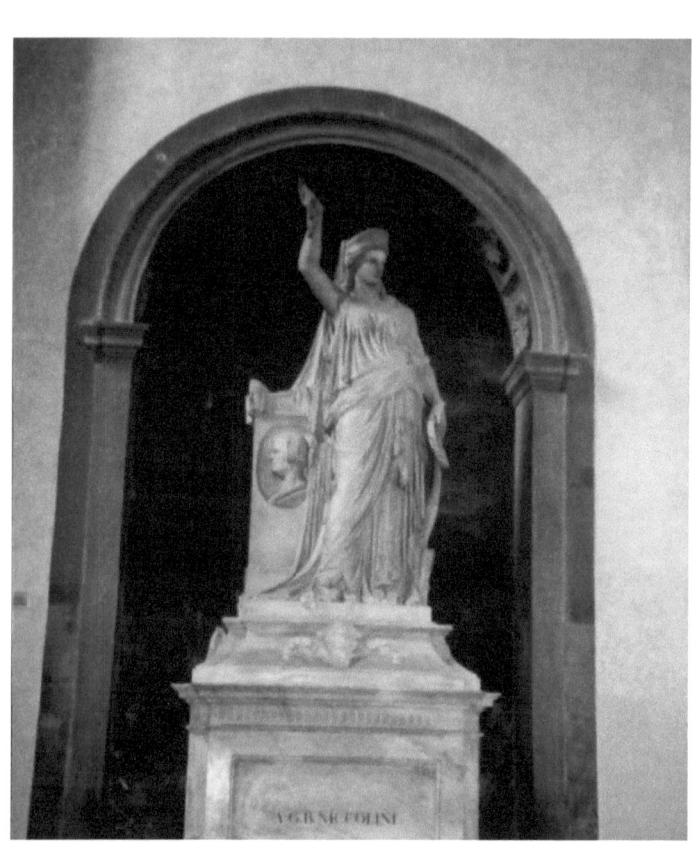

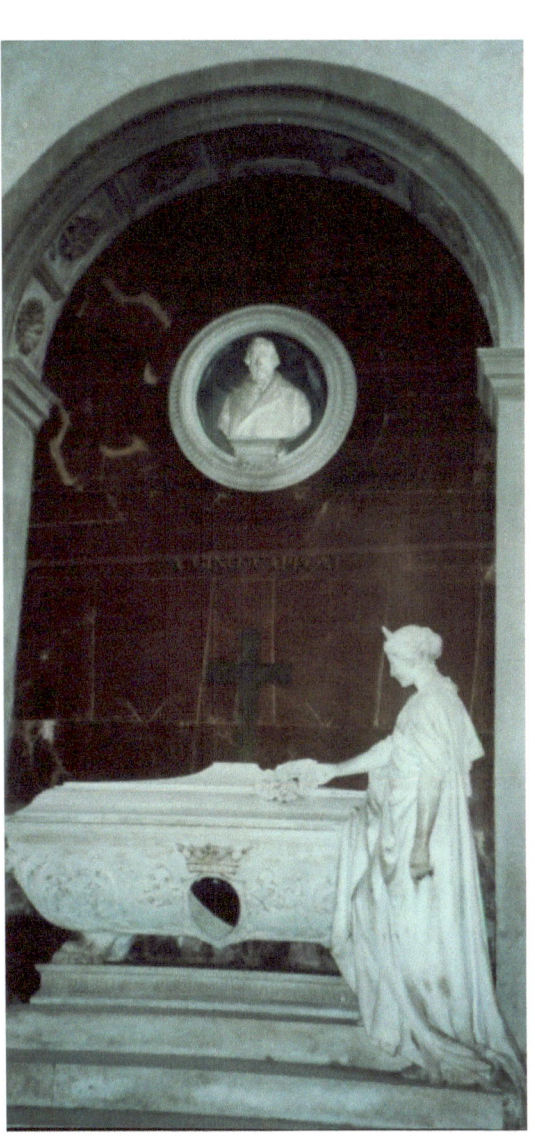

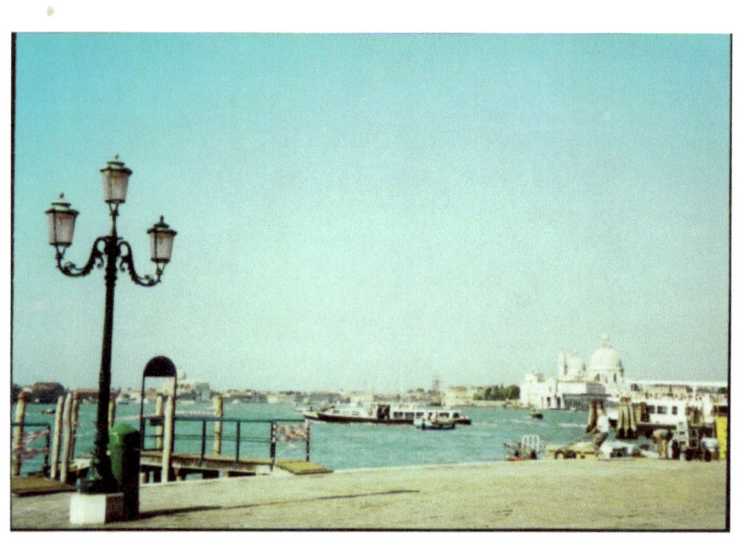

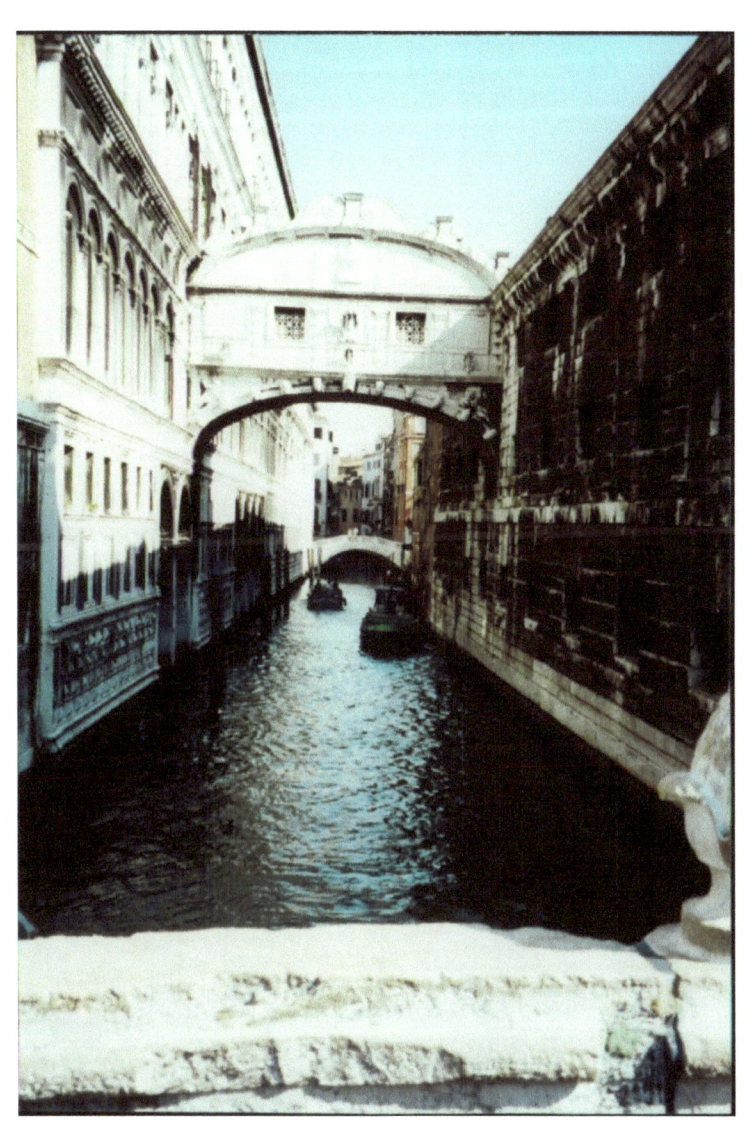

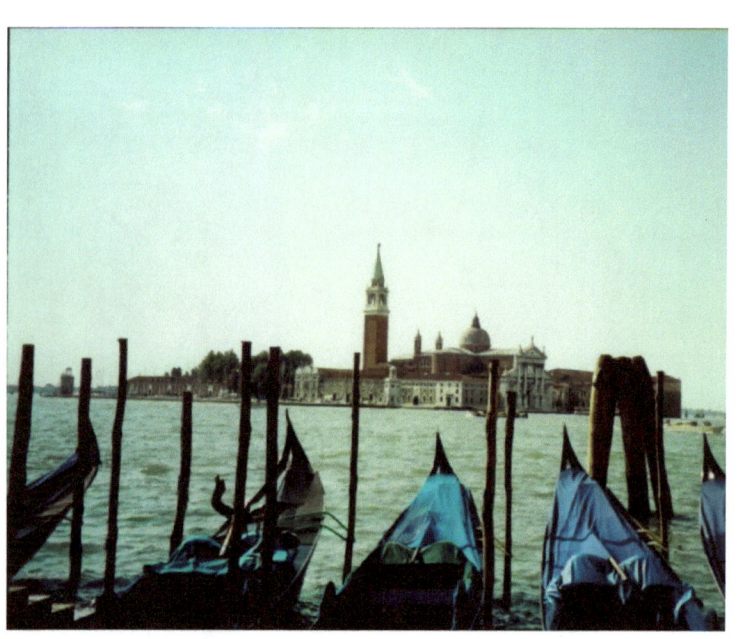

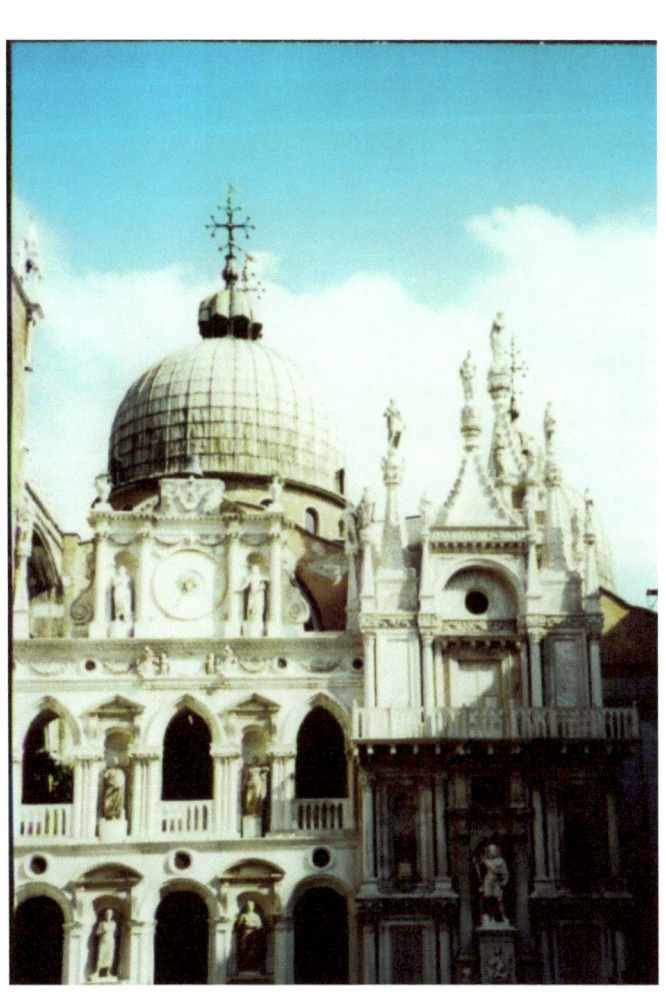

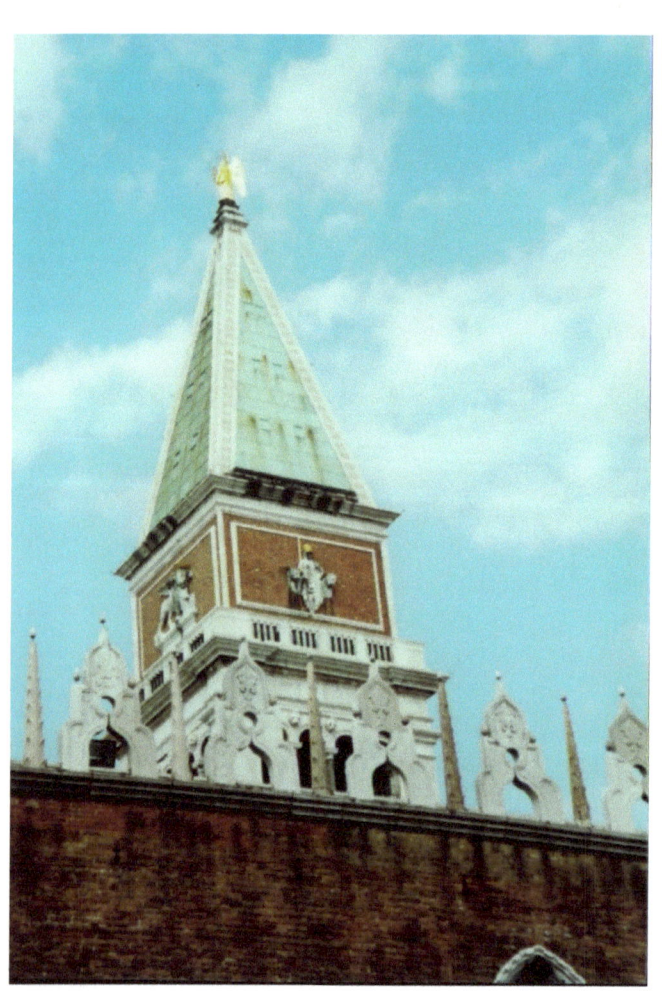

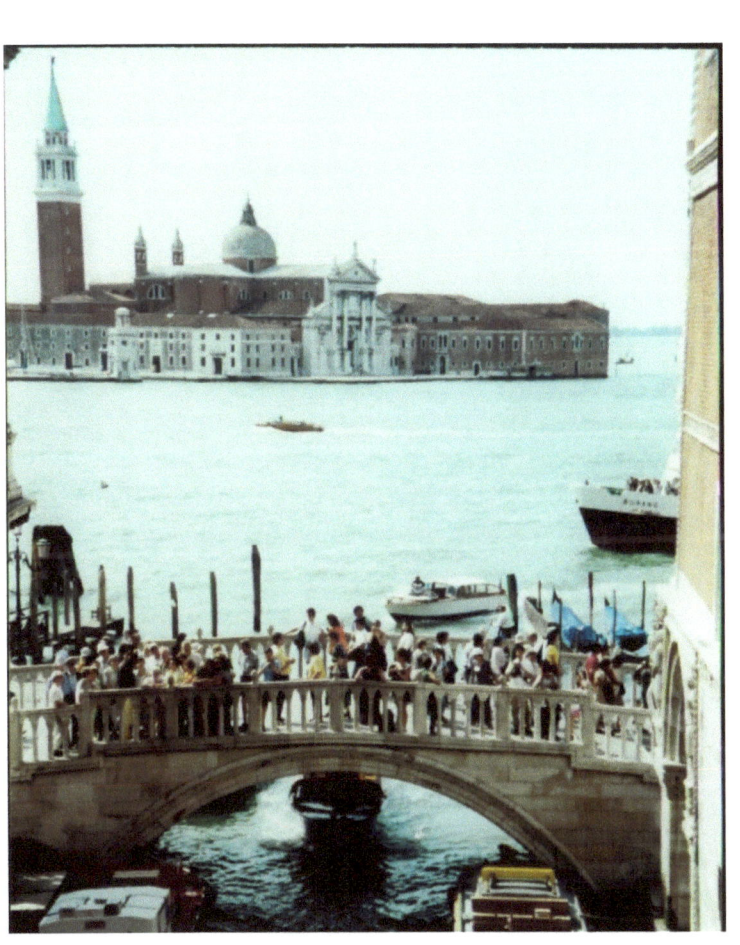

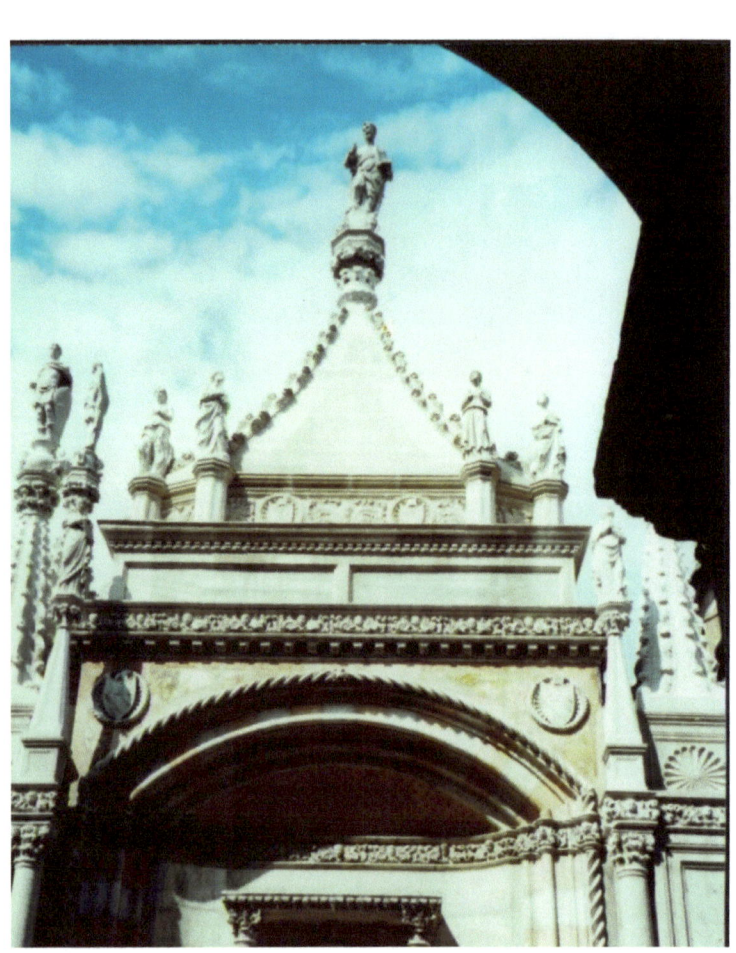

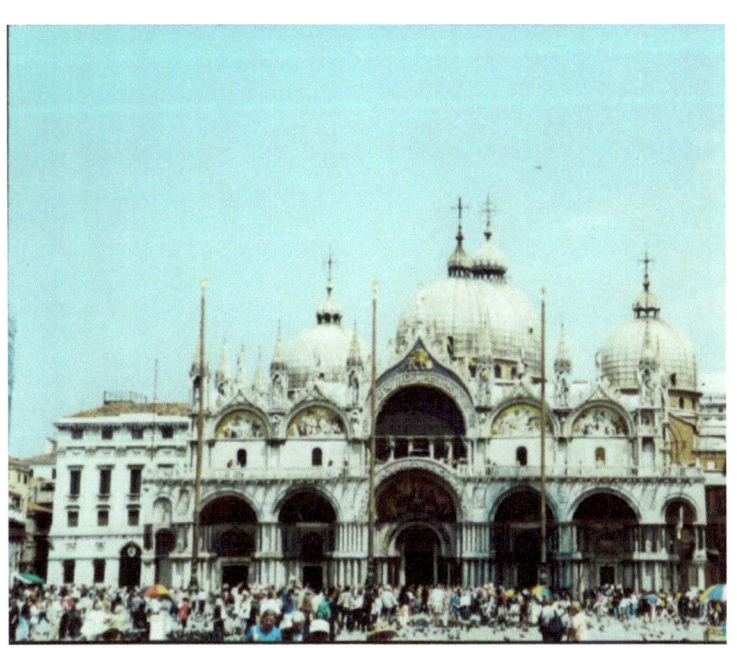

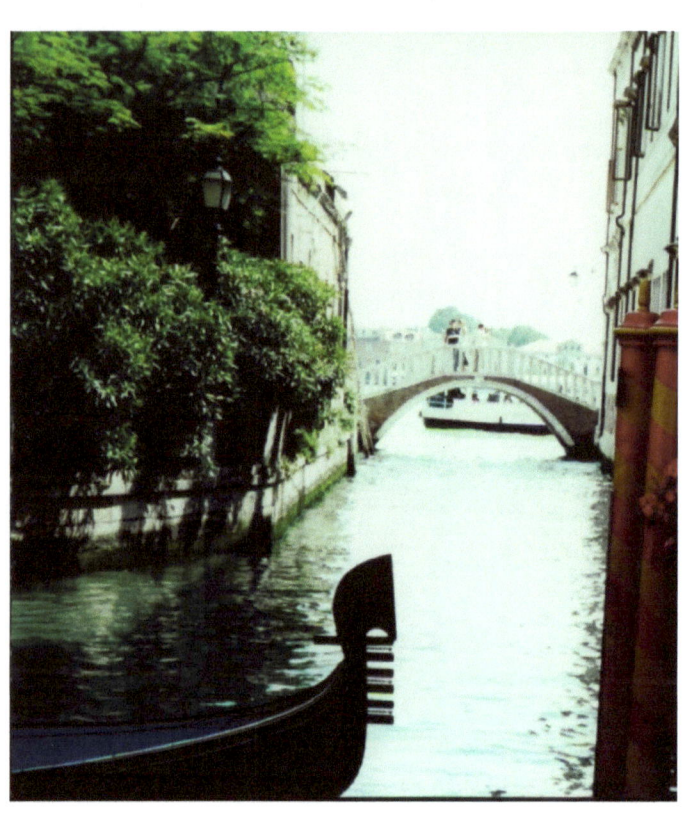

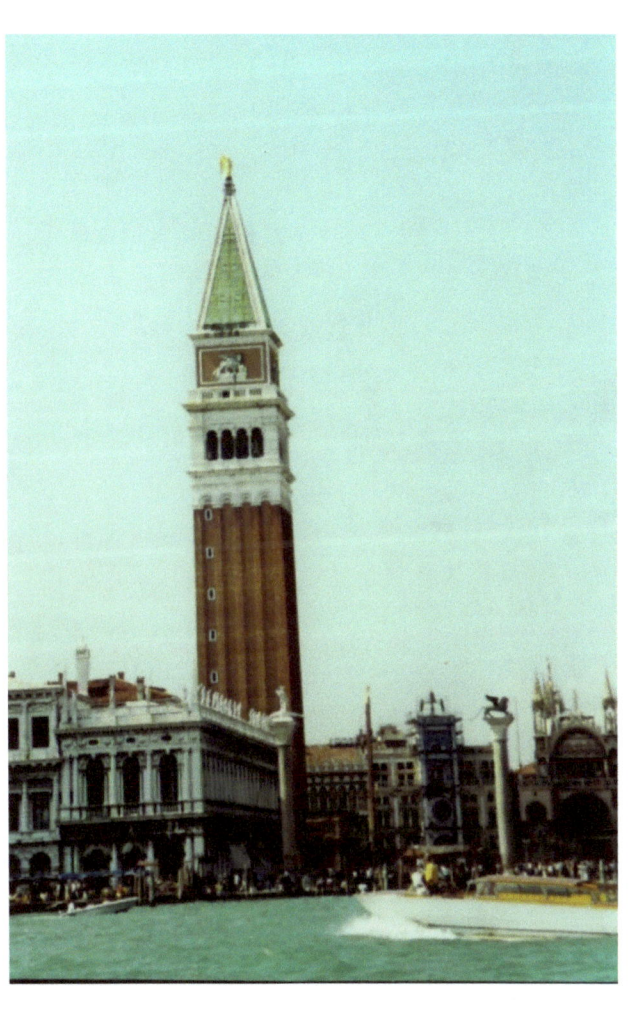

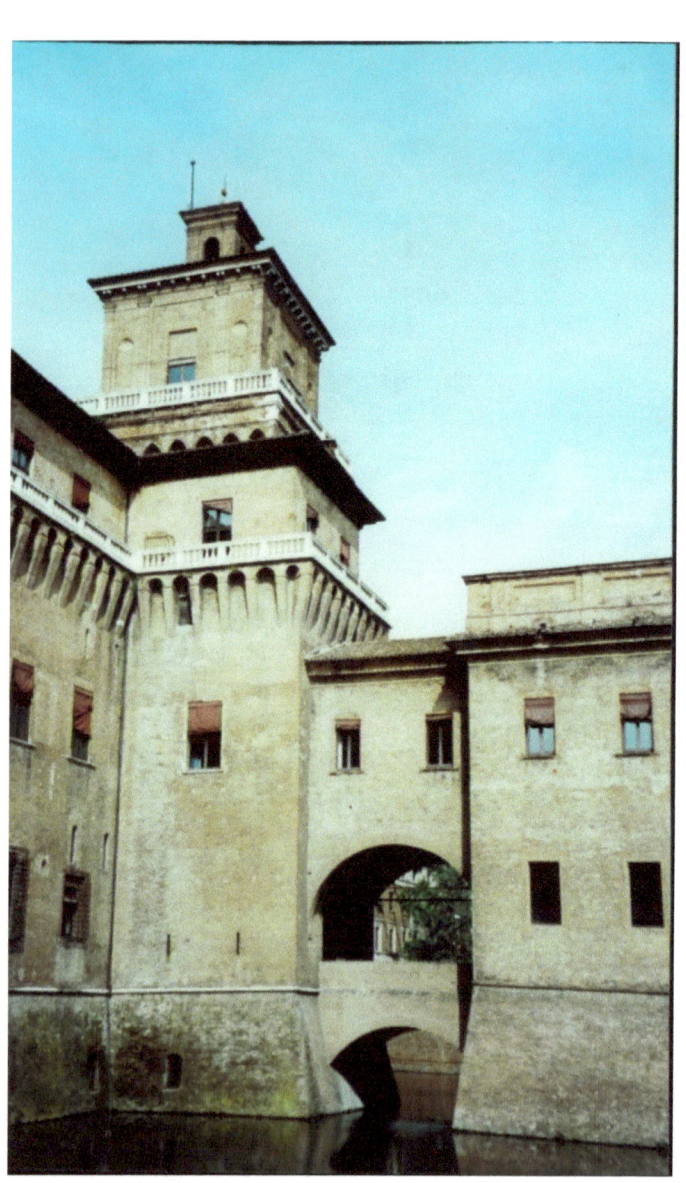

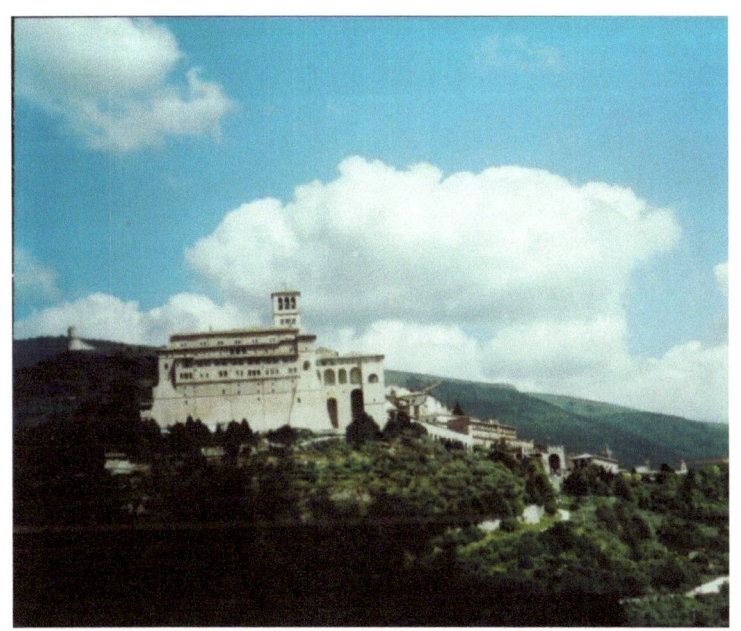

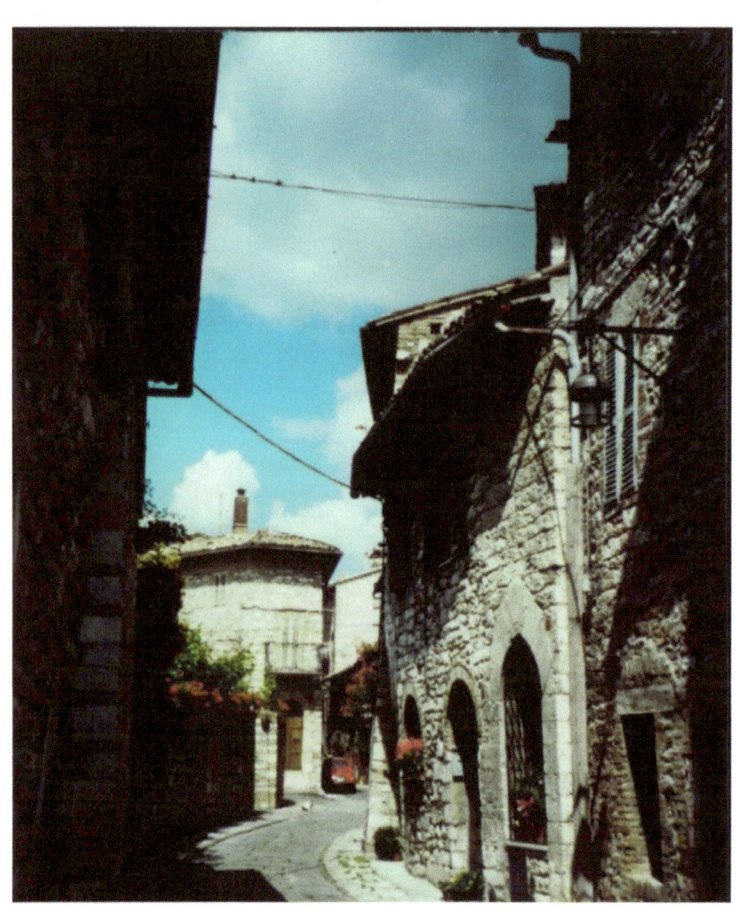

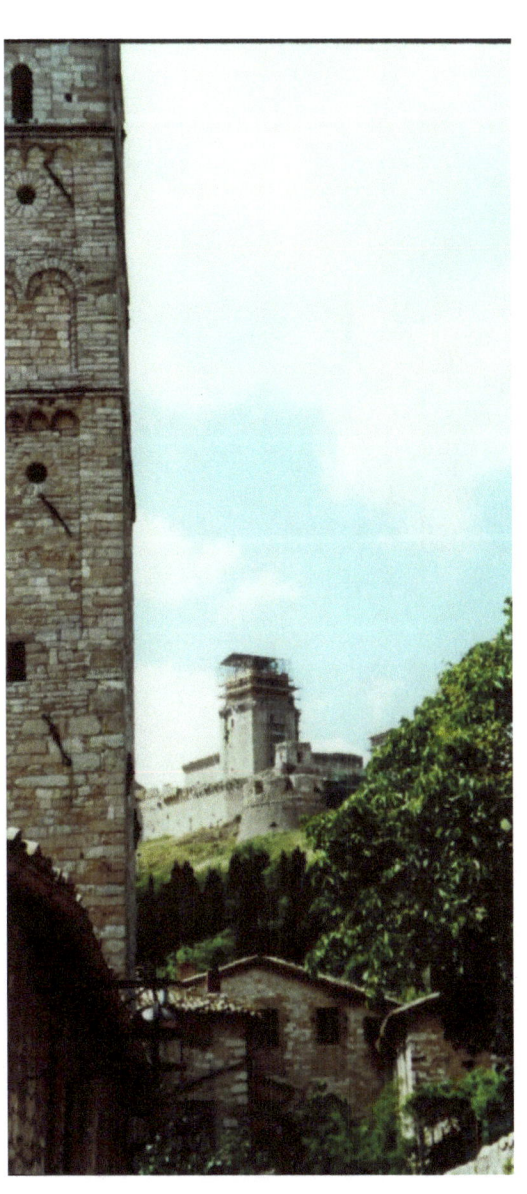

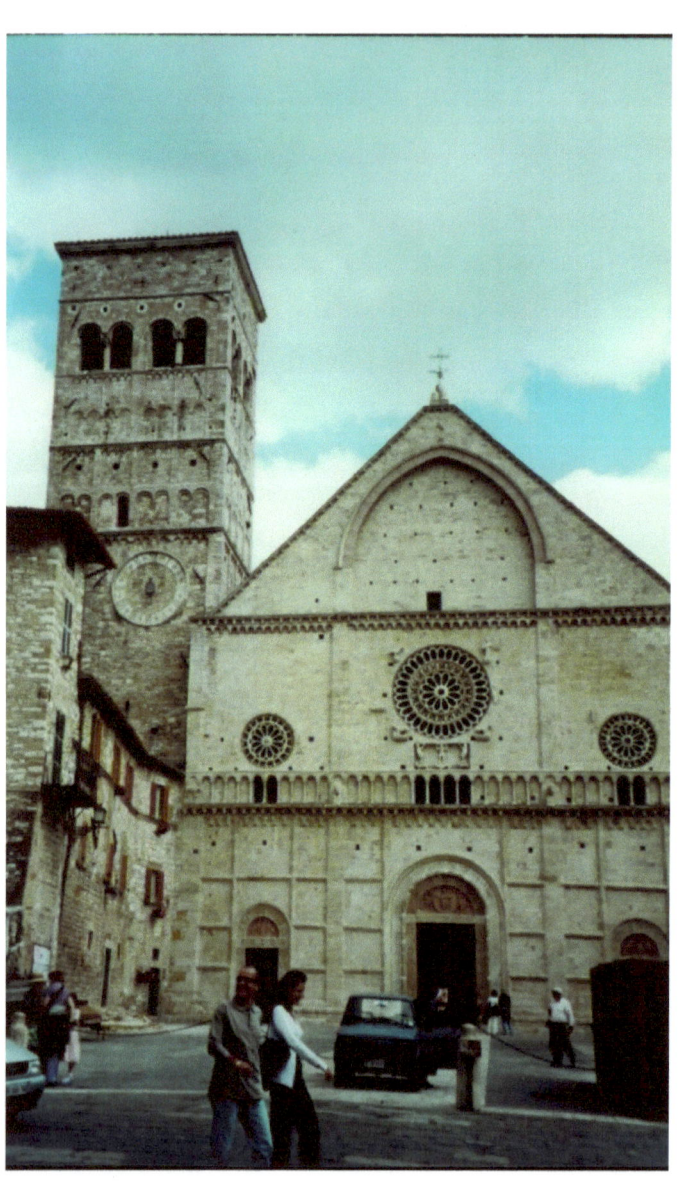

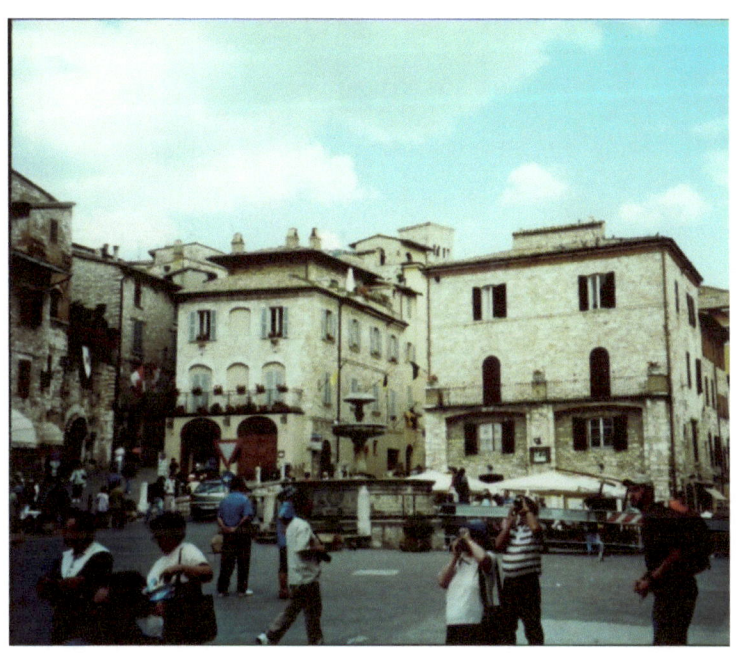

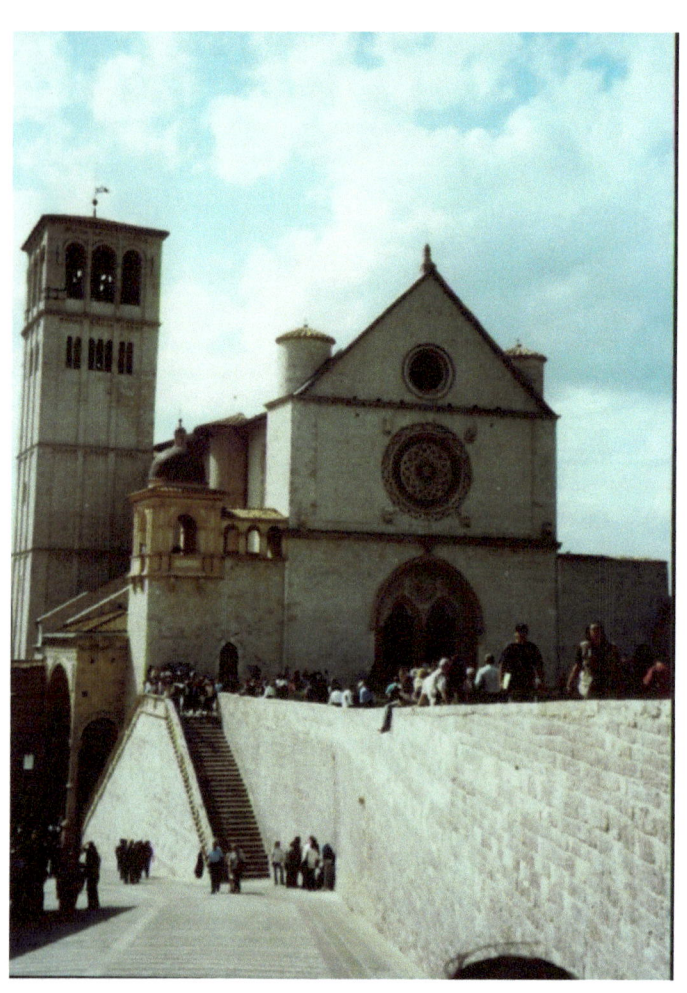

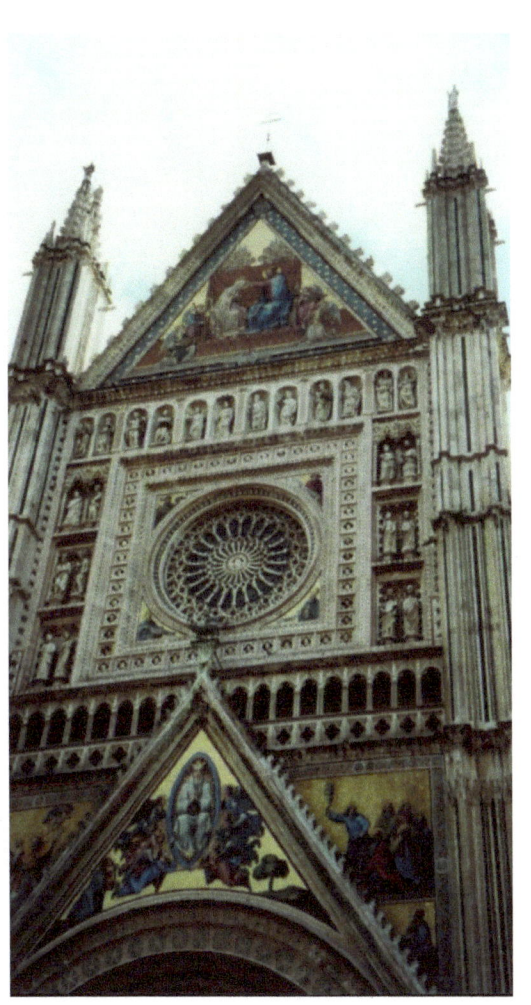

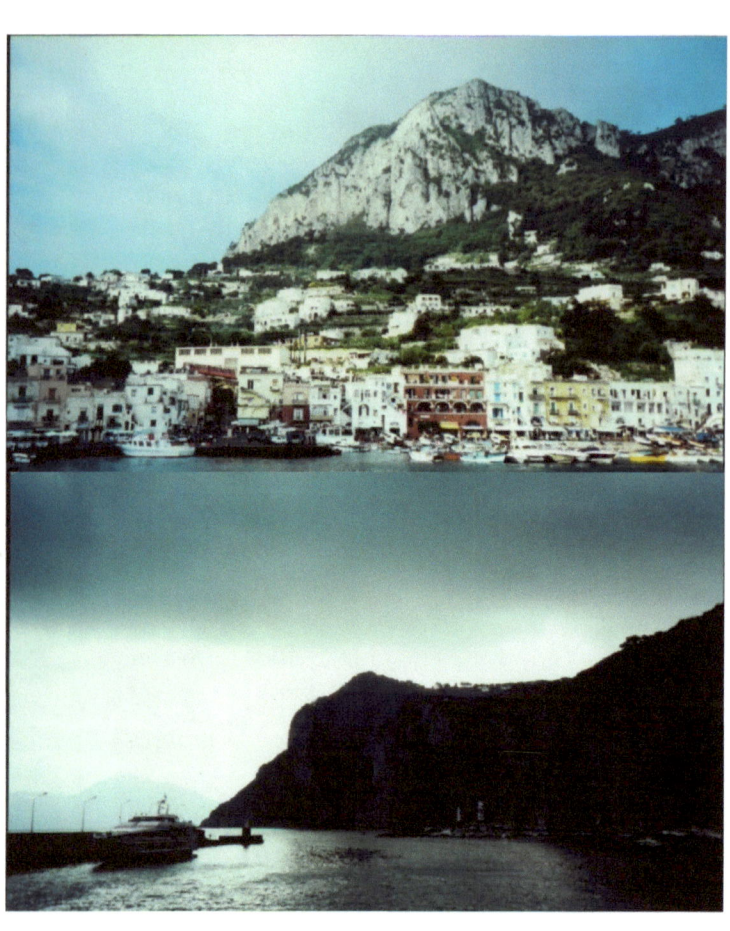

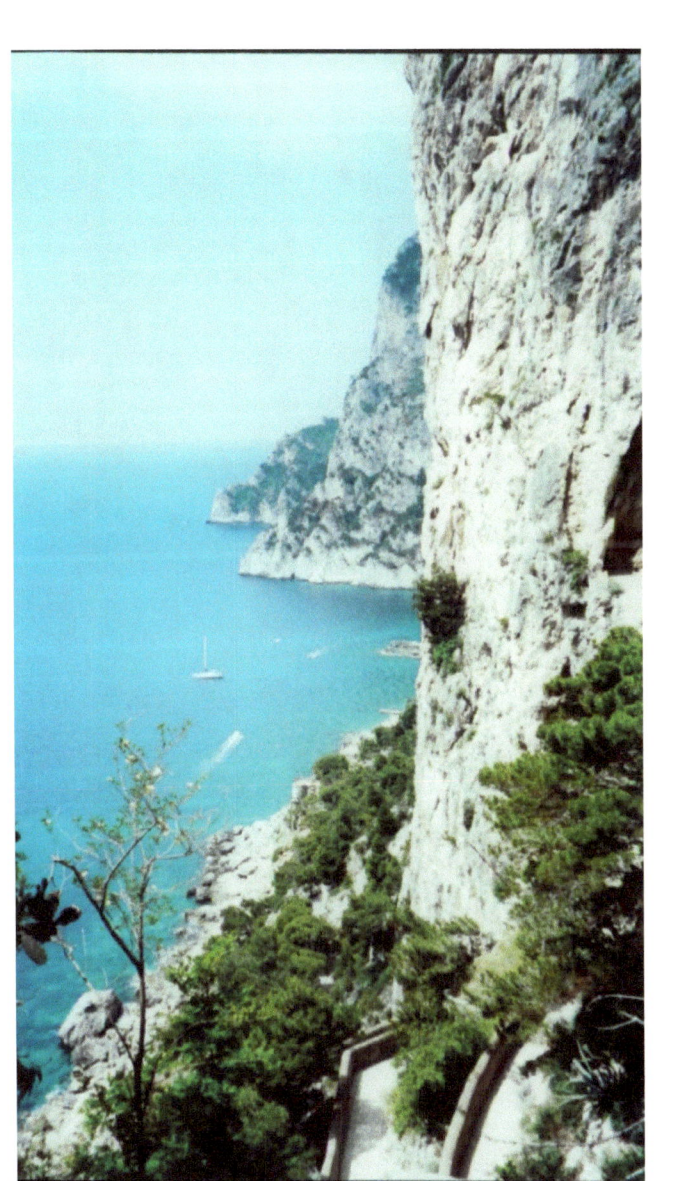

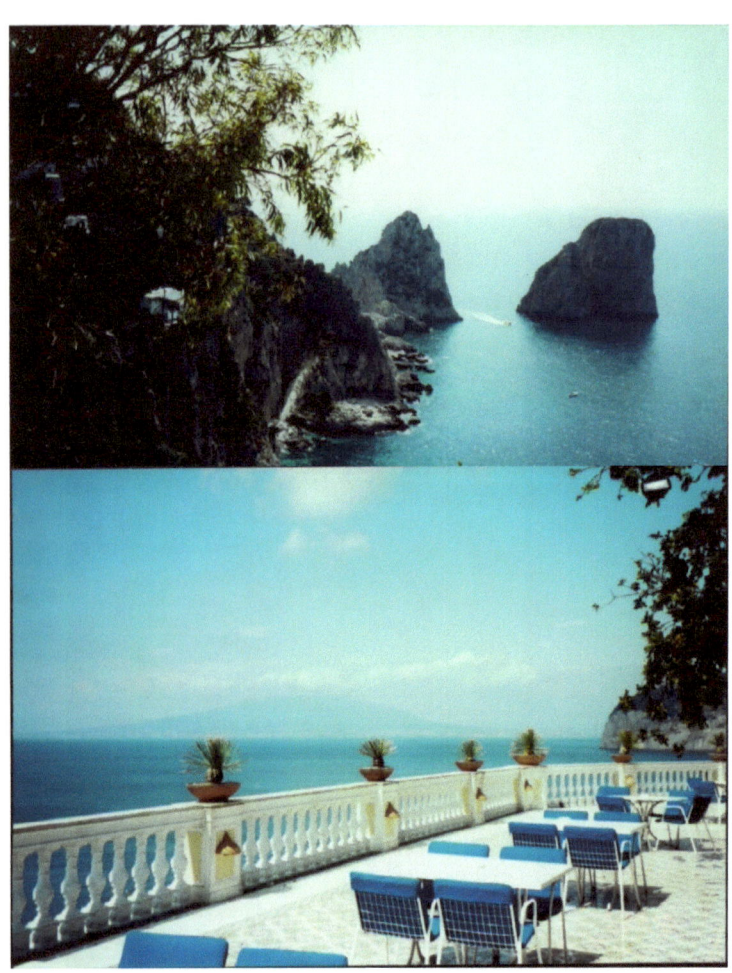

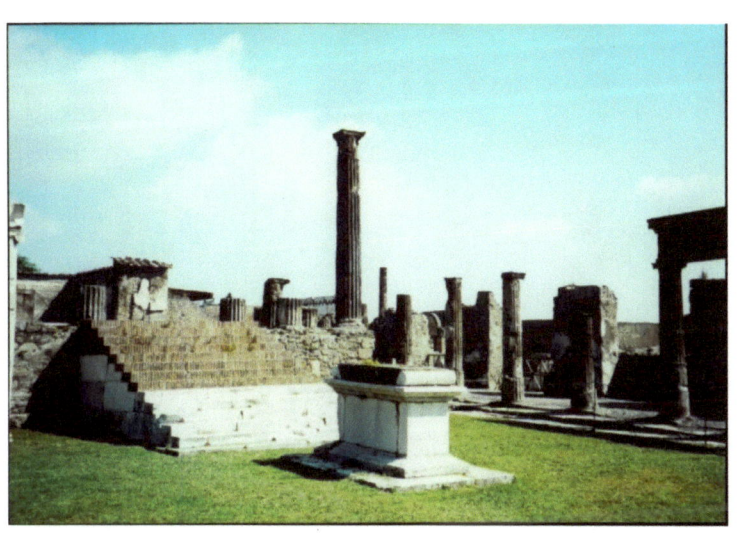

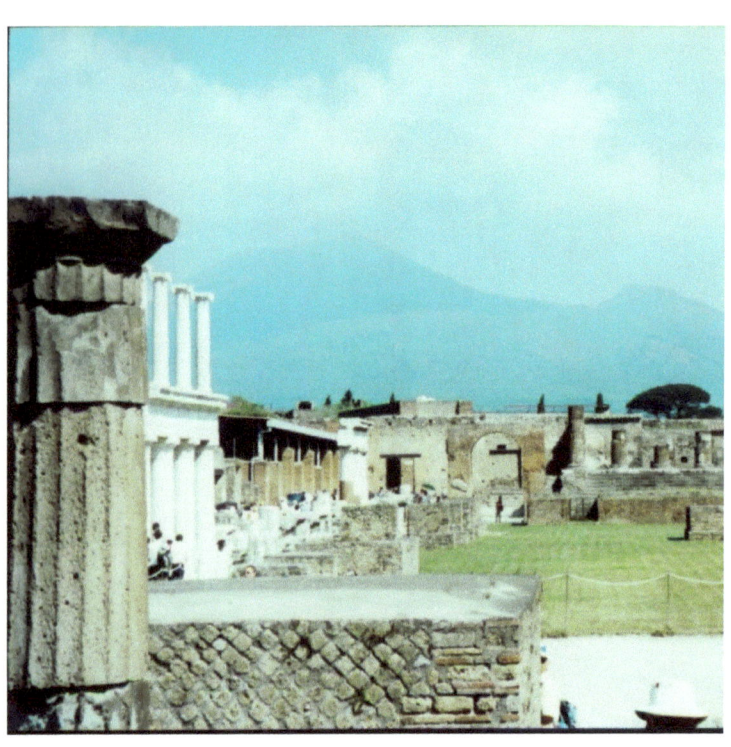

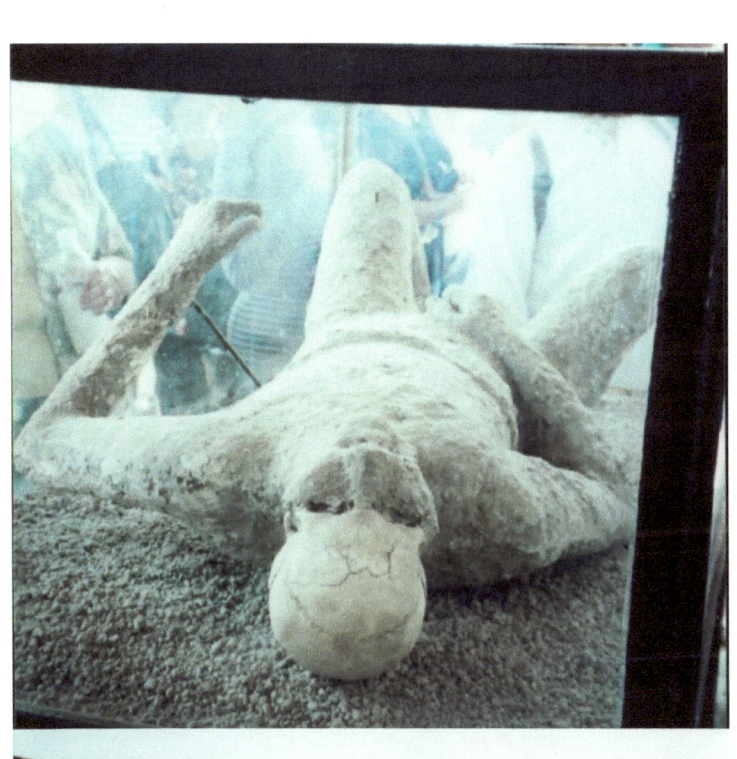

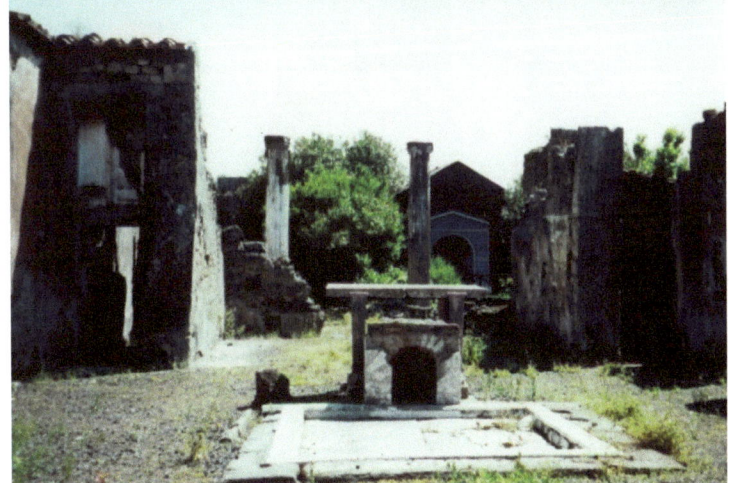

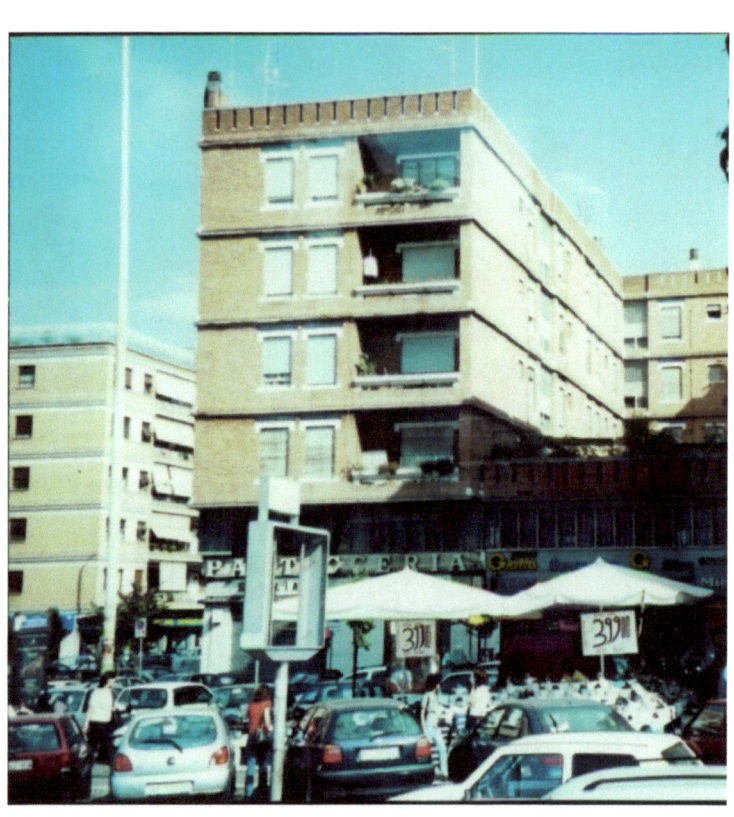

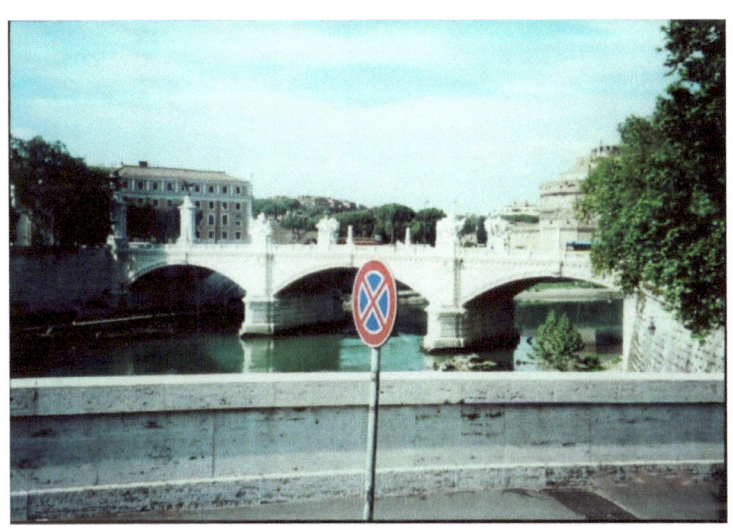

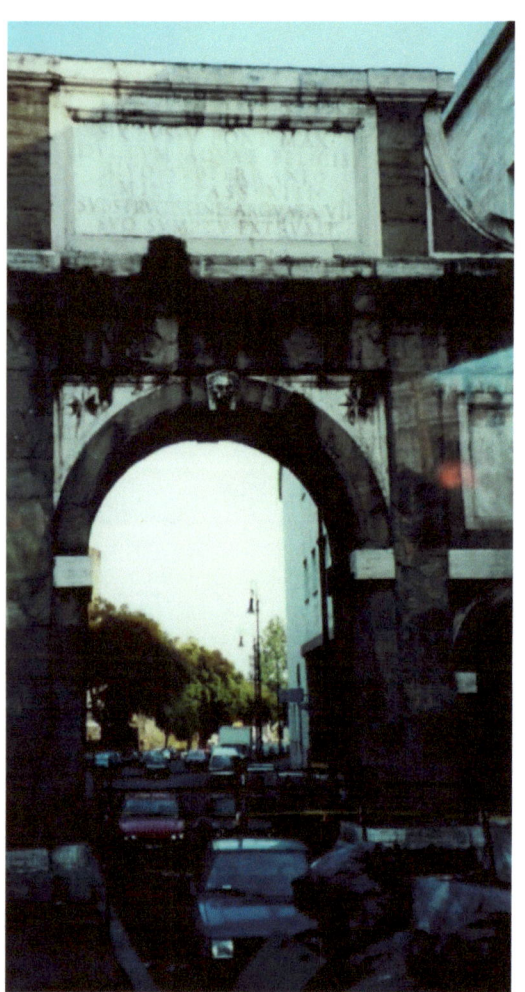

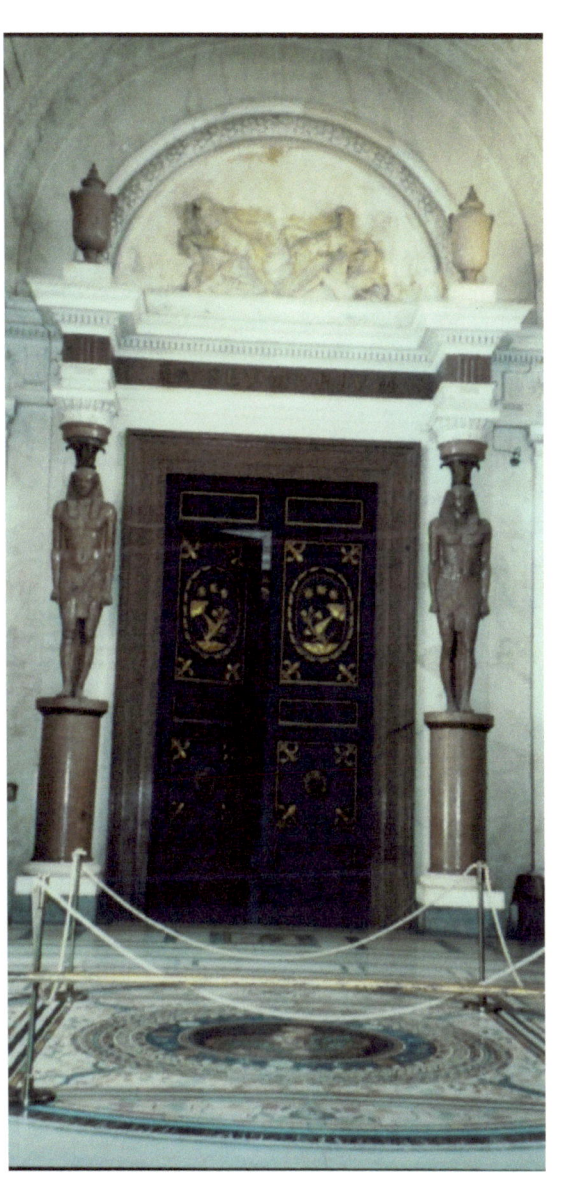

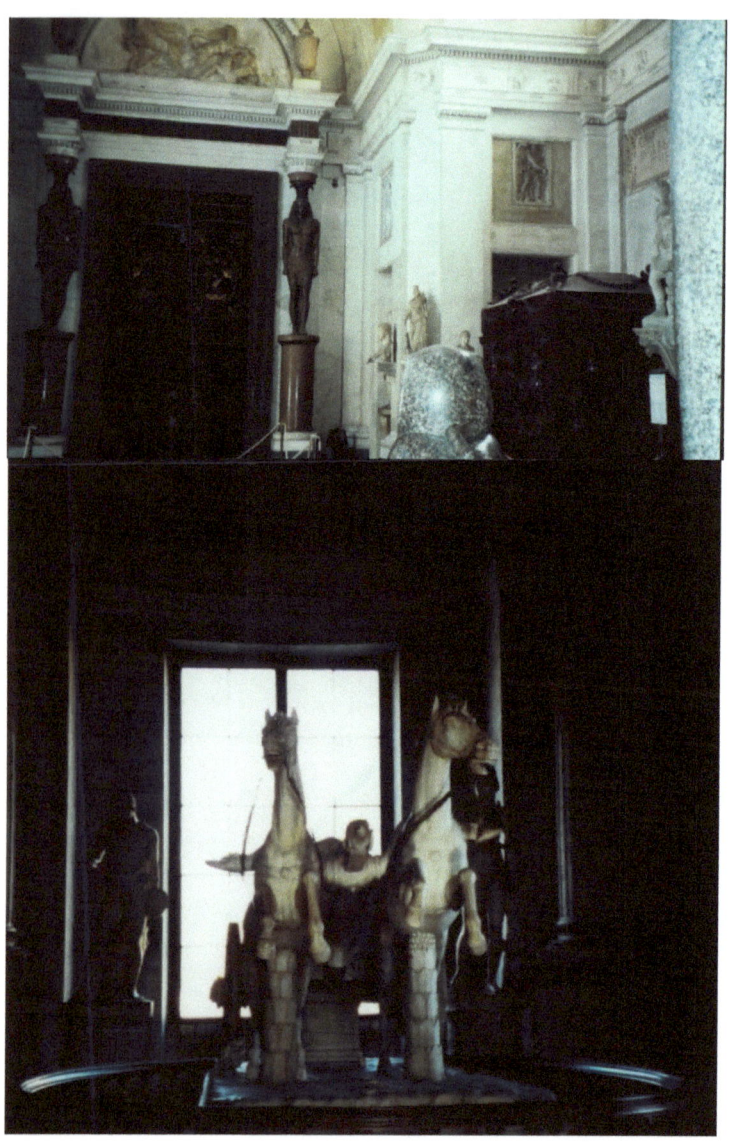

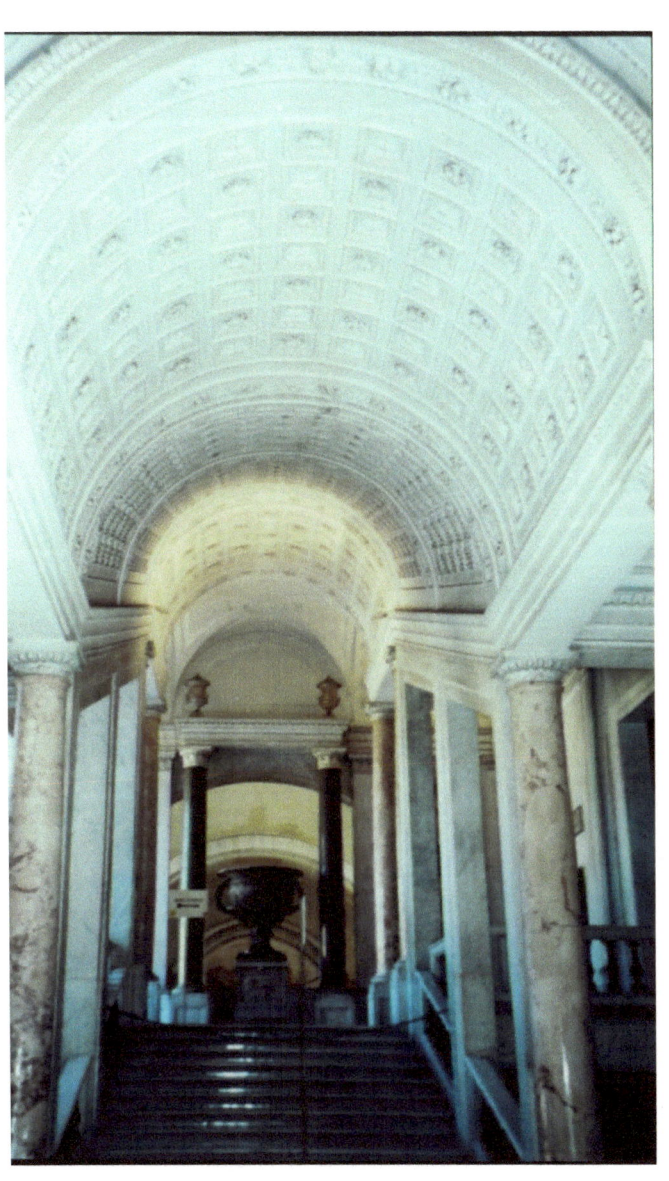

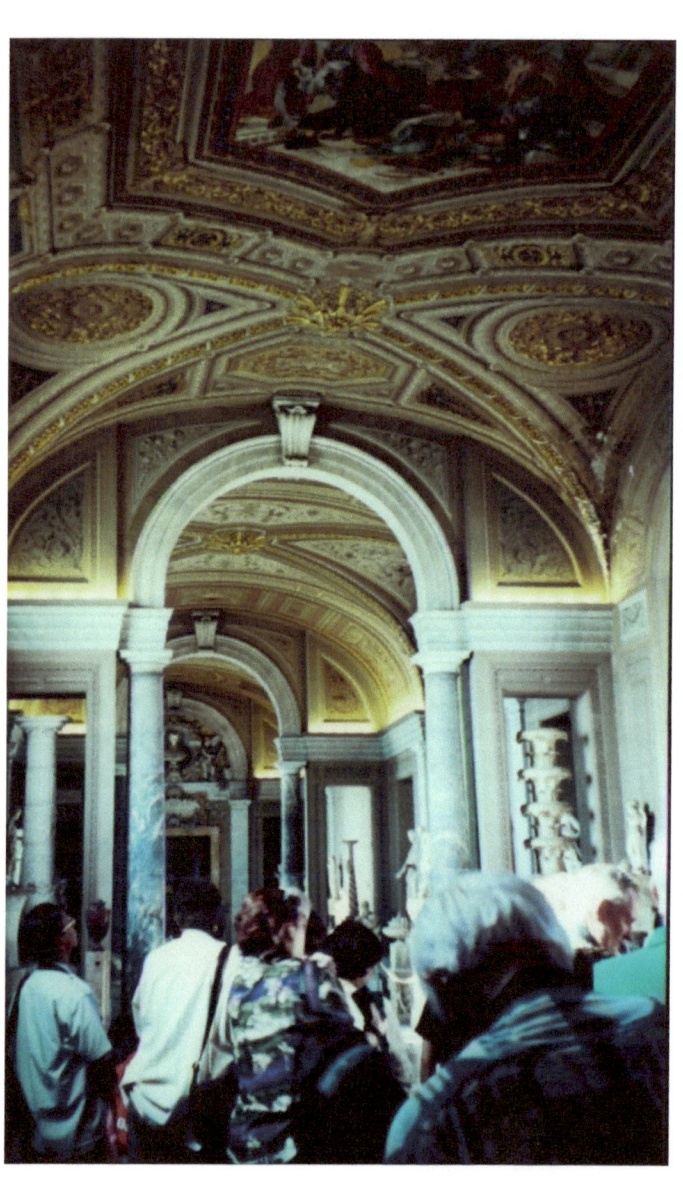

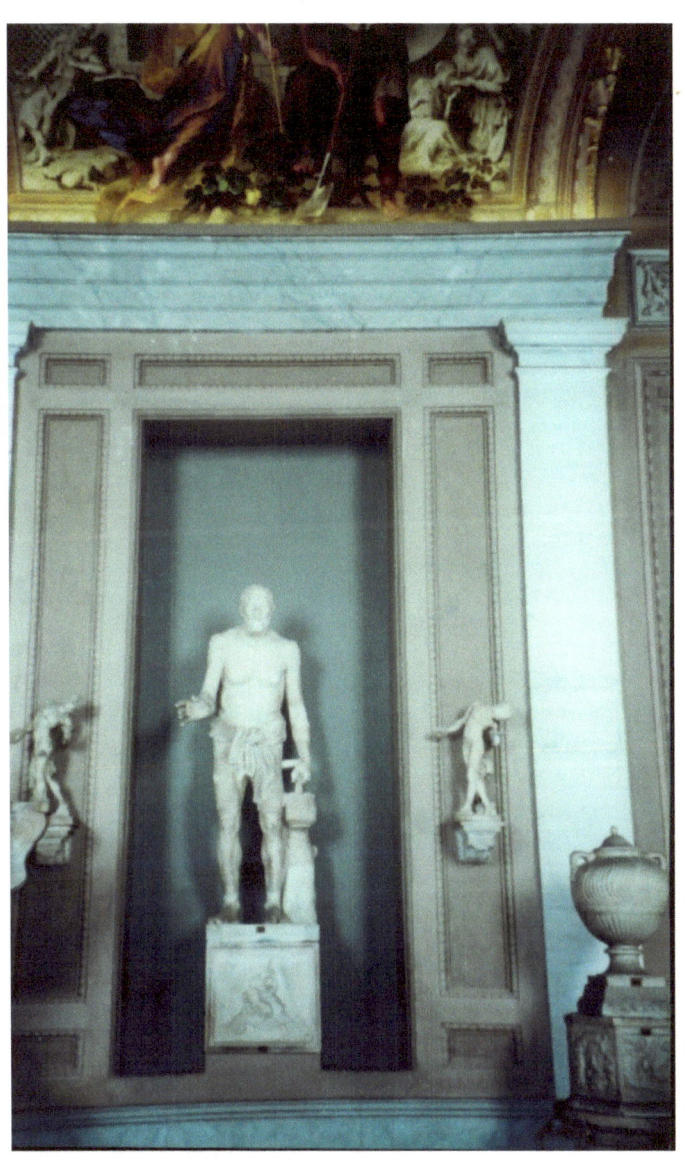

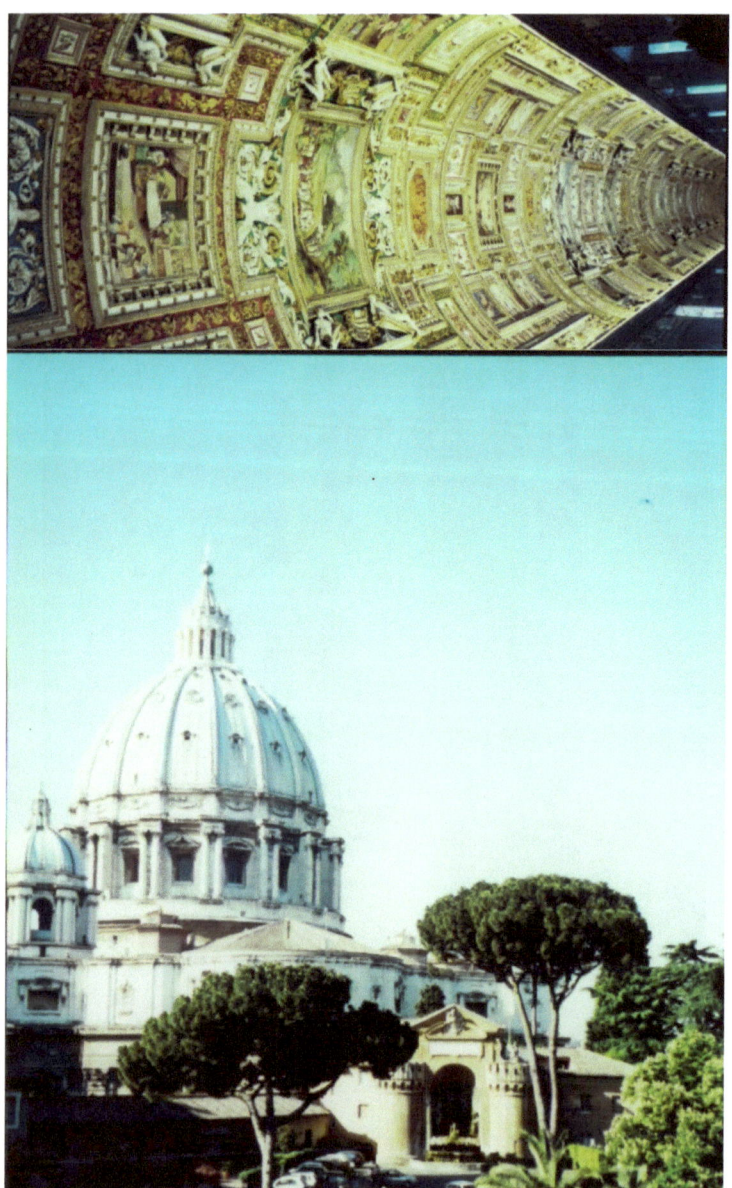

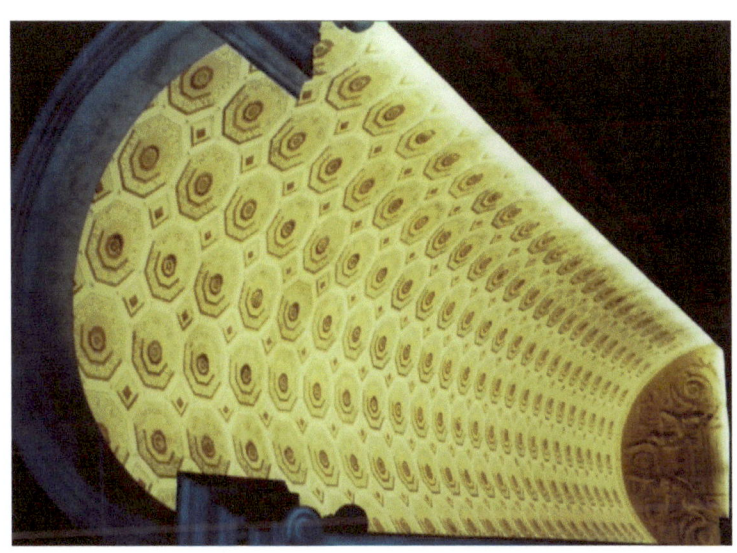

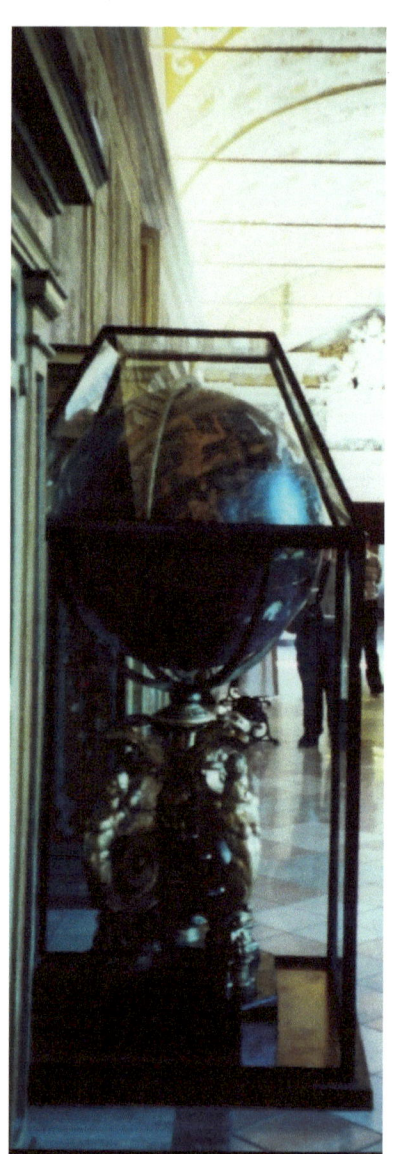

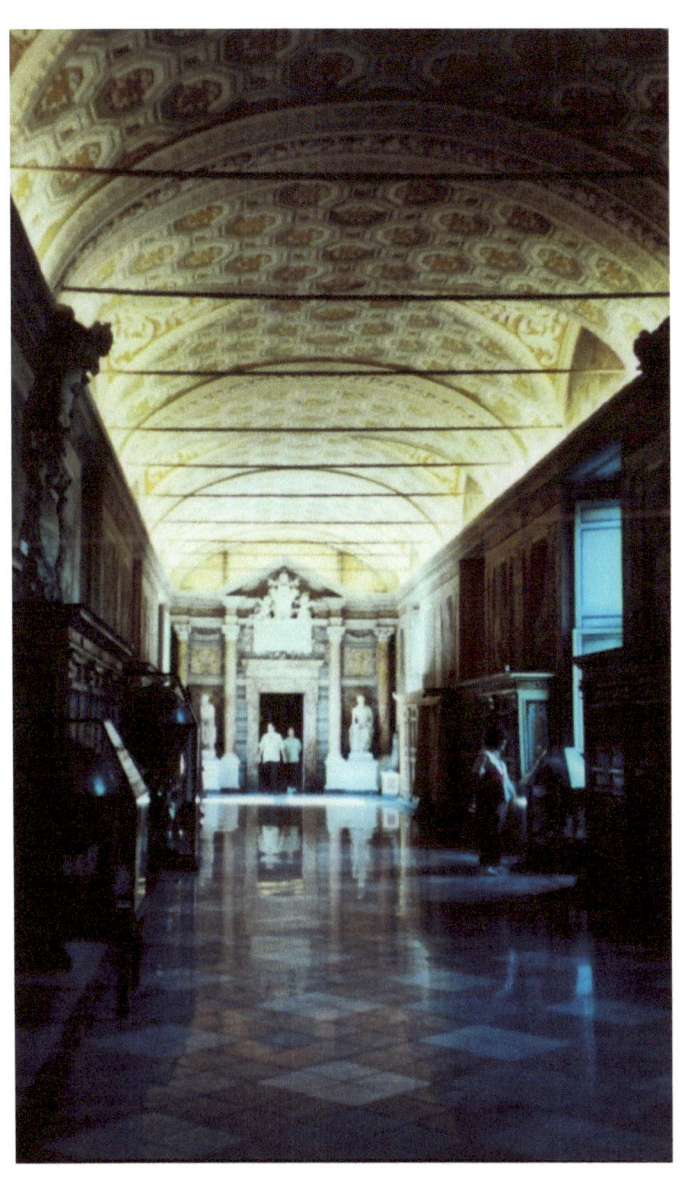

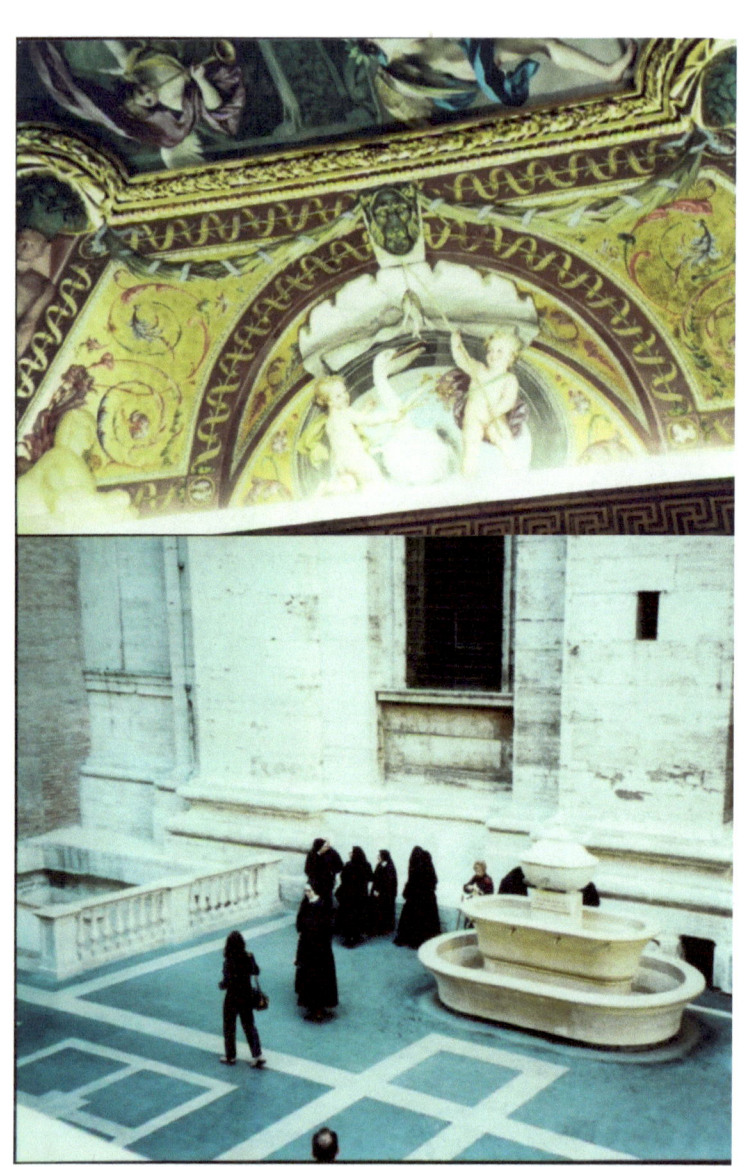

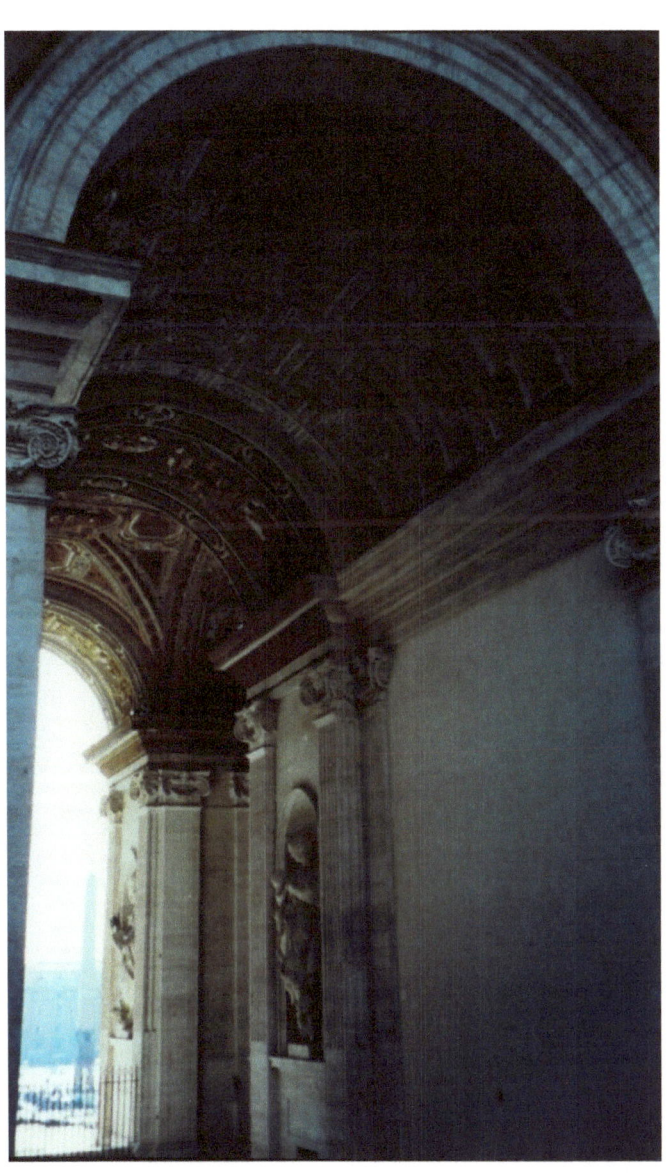

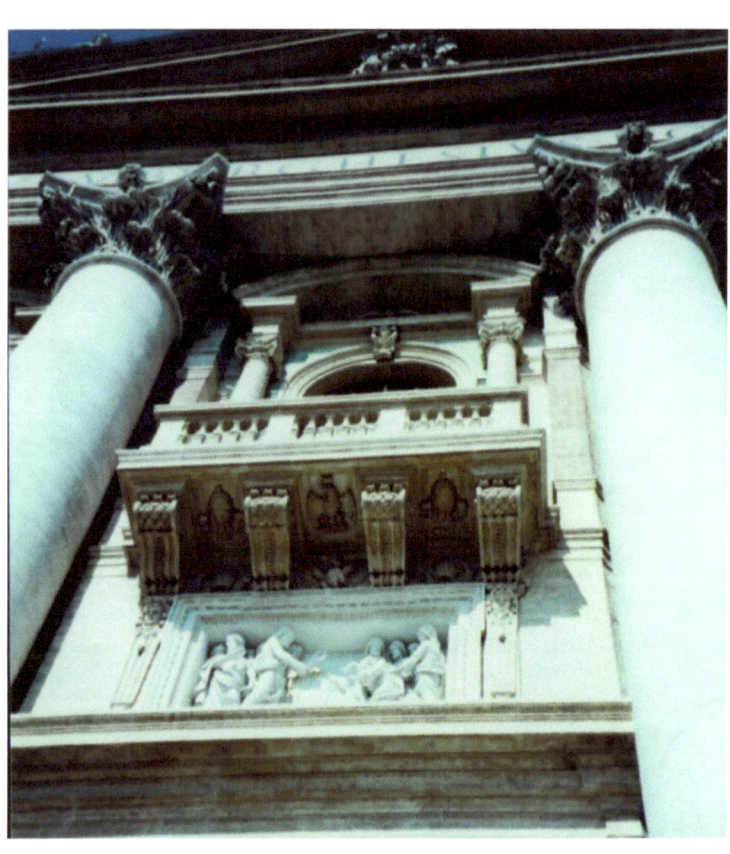

www.ingramcontent.com/pod-product-compliance
Lightning Source LLC
Chambersburg PA
CBHW040810200526
45159CB00022B/202